A LISTENING CHURCH

Autonomy and Communion
in African Churches

Elochukwu E. Uzukwu

Eugene, Oregon

Wipf and Stock Publishers
199 W 8th Ave, Suite 3
Eugene, OR 97401

A Listening Church
Autonomy and Communion in African Churches
By Uzukwu, Elochukwu E.
Copyright©1996 by Uzukwu, Elochukwu E.
ISBN: 1-59752-898-6
Publication date 8/24/2006
Previously published by Orbis Books, 1996

To Engelbert Mveng, S.J., my friend and mentor,
assassinated in April 1995
by those who like to hold the Word captive.

To the hundreds of thousands of defenselesss Rwandan
and other unsung African martyrs
of this end of the twentieth century.

May your blood be the seed of new life in Africa!

Contents

Acknowledgments

Early in the year 1994, when winter was waning in Europe, I was invited to teach a course on "Trends in African Theology" by the Institut Catholique of Paris. At that time, the Special Assembly of the Synod of Bishops for Africa was about to begin. Apart from a detailed treatment of the varieties of theological effort in Africa, I added a short section to my course outline on emergent African ecclesiology. This book is a product of the discussions and reflections on that part of my course. The metaphor of "church-as-family" suggested by the synod enriched our class discussions. I thank my students, Africans and Europeans, for their participation and the crucial questions they raised about Africa and her future. I also thank the outgoing dean of theology, Joseph Doré, and the superior of the French Spiritans, Jean-Paul Hoch, for inviting me to teach at the Institut de Science et de Théologie des Religions (ISTR). The head of the ISTR, Jean Joncheray, and my confrère Paul Coulon made critical remarks on the course and especially on the section dealing with a relevant ecclesiology. I am very grateful to them. I thank also my confrère and elder Joseph Gross, the editor of *Spiritus,* who initiated the project of having an African Spiritan teach a missiology course at the ISTR. My former provincial superior, Alex Ekechukwu, his successor, Mike Onwuemelie, and my colleagues at the Spiritan International School of Theology (SIST), Attakwu, Enugu, gave their full support to my visiting lectureship at the ISTR.

Before the Synod for Africa opened, the Rwandan massacres hit the world with all their diabolic violence. Reactions moved from shock to blame, to action programs to stop the massacres and to alleviate the suffering of the refugees, then to critical assessment of responsibility, and so on. Africans in France and elsewhere in Europe, including the assembled bishops at the synod, were challenged to respond to and reflect on this clear regress into barbarism and primitivity. I participated in postsynodal conferences organized in Tübingen and Rennes.

My interventions in those conferences addressed the Rwandan tragedy and the phenomenon of African dictatorships through my proposal of a viable way of building a humane society in Africa and an emergent African ecclesiology. I thank the organizers of the conferences, the Kindugu group in Tübingen and the Spiritans in Rennes, for inviting me to participate in the discussions.

After his official visitation of Nigeria in early 1994, Pierre Schouver, the superior general of the Spiritans (Holy Ghost Fathers and Brothers), was kind enough to share his impressions with me. In the course of our discussion the issue of the organization of African societies and the influence these should have in the renewal of the church came up. I learned from him that the totem of the Manja chief is the rabbit because it has large ears. The chief is one who is versed in the art of listening. I have utilized this imagery in this book according to my particular style and for my purpose. I am grateful to Pierre Schouver for this information, which I consider vital in writing this book.

The SEDOS Documentation and Research Centre in Rome gave me free access to its library in the summer of 1994. I am grateful to Walter von Holzen, the director of SEDOS, and his staff for their hospitality. My colleagues in the Spiritan School of Philosophy Isienu (Remy Onyewuenyi, Oliver Iwuchukwu, and Chuka Obi) read parts of the manuscripts and made helpful remarks. Also my friend and colleague, Breifne Walker, here in SIST, and my revered elder brother R. C. Arazu read most of the chapters and made their critical remarks. Cora Twohig-Moengangongo, my other feminist colleague and friend at SIST, made useful comments on certain sections of this book. I am very grateful to all of them. I am also indebted to Juliana Itodo, who spent additional hours to print out the many versions of this book.

I benefited from the comments and critical remarks of the editor at Orbis Books (Susan Perry) and from two Orbis assessors (Anthony Gittins and Laurenti Magesa). I am very grateful to Orbis for accepting my manuscript.

The content and tone of this book come totally from me. My analysis of African history from the point of view of the victims and my preference of the ecclesiology of the North African church are my personal way of reflecting on a church which is One but Many.

CHAPTER 1

African Reality and African Theology

Africa—the Face with Many Scars

Africa is seen today in the world community as a continent of misery. Many statistics trumpet this reality. Ecological disasters, such as flood and drought, bring agricultural production in many regions of the continent to a standstill. Warring groups prevent farmers from cultivating fertile land. Africa can no longer feed its teeming millions. Economic depression of unparalleled proportions makes existing authoritarian regimes more repressive. Dictatorships and civil wars uproot women, men, and children from ancestral homes to neighboring countries. In Sierra Leone, Somalia, Sudan, Angola, and Liberia it is difficult to silence the guns. In Rwanda and Burundi ethnic strife makes it impossible for the BaHutu and BaTutsi to live in peace. Machetes, den-guns, and automatic rifles are freely used in the barbaric massacre of hundreds of thousands of children, women, and men. Even the Kokumba and Namumba of Ghana and Togo settle scores which have been simmering since the abolition of the slave trade. Refugees in Africa number over seven million; that is about 50 percent of the world population of refugees.

Intellectuals whose role in the development of culture is irreplaceable are driven away from their homeland or flee the shores of Africa for greener pastures abroad (the brain drain). African dictators, like their ilk elsewhere in the world, are intolerant of a free press and a vocal opposition. Disease plagues those uprooted from their homes as well as those who live in relative peace. Malaria is still the greatest killer. Infant mortality is very high. The plague of AIDS invades cities

1

and villages. One out of every forty Africans is supposedly a carrier. Those who escape disease may not escape criminals. There is hardly any cause for cheer.

The criteria set by the World Bank for relatively good governance are banished from most regions of Africa. Legitimacy, responsibility, and the equitable redistribution of wealth are a luxury. This same financial institution supervises the open-market economy, deregulation, and devaluation of the weak currencies in the weak and extroverted economies of Africa! For example, the Republic of Niger is one of the countries reputedly doing well in Sahelian Africa. In 1993 it had a net import of US$320,000,000 as against a net export of US$290,000,000. Consequently, it had a deficit budget. With the 50 percent devaluation of the CFA franc one does not need a soothsayer to foretell doom.[1]

This is the wounded face of Africa frequently portrayed in the mass media, a media controlled by Western conglomerates. Apart from sports and music one hardly hears any positive news item about Africa. For their part, when Africans narrate their plight in these trying times, they sound even more pessimistic. The marginalized elite who fled their countries to maintain a relatively decent living abroad make uncomplimentary comparisons between their host countries and their fatherland. Government employees in the Benin Republic and Nigeria whose salaries remained unpaid for months or years have nothing but spite for their governments. Even the members of the defunct national assembly in Nigeria (disbanded by the military coup of November 1993) lampoon their colleagues and the military usurpers. The indigenous business community, such as the Manufacturers Association of Nigeria, makes no predictions for better cheer.

African Theology Responds to the Crisis

This image of apparent hopelessness, shared both by foreign friends and foes and by the daughters and sons of Africa, is disturbing. No continent or nation may survive or arise from the embers of such pessimism. Theology in Africa takes seriously this situation of misery and oppression as a context for its reflection. It does not adopt the simplistic approach of wishing our problems away, nor simply of denouncing the perpetrators of the evil. Rather, contextual theology in Africa tries to propose viable models for the reconstruction of our societies.[2]

African theology of liberation has raised its voice, since the 1980s, to denounce the misery that besets our people and to identify the root causes of our crisis. It tries to trace the historical origin of our burden from the time of slavery through colonialism to independence. But it avoids the naiveté of simply blaming the past. Rather it calls for a dynamic, as opposed to an archaeological, reading of the social history of African societies, an approach which emphasizes the fundamental element of change and development in African history and traditions. It calls for a church which is committed to the social transformation of Africa and leads by example—a church which is, for example, self-reliant at all levels. Similarly, black theology of South Africa denounces apartheid and the state religion which supports it. Apartheid is demonic. The theology of the Dutch Reformed Church which supports it is a heresy. Black theology in South Africa is developed by blacks under oppression. The successful dethronement of the South African apartheid regime through local and international struggle is a clear sign of hope that an alternative society is possible in our continent.

But in order to combat our pessimism, our misery, and our oppression, foreign or local, and to reconstruct in an enduring way, we must learn to depend fully on our own resources, without being the less attentive to the realities of a modern world and a global village. The church, aided by the reflection of her theologians, will become a more credible agent of change when Christian life emerges from the realities of the African context and Christian theology responds to questions posed by the context and is nourished by local resources. These resources are derived from the social, political, economic, and religious values which have been sustaining African communities as they face change and development in their encounter with the realities of the modern world.

Points of Hope—New Point of Departure

Africa is not a complete story of hopelessness. In many villages the colonial structures have not totally disrupted African traditional patterns of social organization. Some ethnic groups, such as the Yoruba of Nigeria and the Bamileke of Cameroon, maintain the fundamental aspects of their traditional culture while being nonetheless modern. But the cultural option of the Massaï of Eastern Africa, which rejects modernity in an attempt to preserve its traditional way of life, appears to represent the extreme end of the spectrum. In cities and villages deeply transformed by modern Western culture (in areas of communication, government, economy, health care delivery, and religion) clan links are still maintained for identity. Traditional rituals of marriage, birth, or death and especially traditional health care are retained.

It is, however, on the level of religious practice that a reaffirmation and modernization or updating of cultural values are most apparent. The practice of various versions of Christianity (by the mainline churches, independent churches, fundamentalist sects, or new religious movements) manifests an inclination toward giving religious solutions to social, economic, and political problems. Some social scientists have called this the search for security.[3] But it is a search which in many ways has opted for the path of the reaffirmation of identity. It is a way of saying that, for the majority of Africans, the integral well-being of humans in this world is seen as the ultimate reality and meaning. Consequently, Africans are setting aside elements of a foreign view of the world propagated with intensity since the era of colonialism.

The colonial and missionary ideology had as their ultimate aim the changing of the identity of the "colonized" and "evangelized." In those situations where nationalistic and evangelical interests were consciously merged, the deep-seated exploitative colonial program along with the then European prejudice against Africans failed to be lucidly examined by the missionaries. Consequently, the African was treated as having neither culture nor religion nor social, economic, or political values worth preserving. The change of the identity of the African person meant, in practice, the abandonment of the indigenous culture, values, and religion in order to embrace those of the West. Even in those situations where nationalistic and imperialistic motives were discerned by the missionary, the cultural limitations of the time, the evangelical fervor of missionary work, and the genuine belief that the colonial program was economically beneficial for Africans made missionaries silent on colonial exploitation. Many missionaries, however, came in direct conflict with the colonial officials over forced labor and the brutal suppression of local opposition to colonial rule. But most were totally in support of the dethronement of the local religious and cultural values. The success of this enterprise despite stiff opposition all over the continent was phenomenal. Africans not only were converted to Christianity but became co-agents of this transformation. However, the present reaffirmation of our cultural values casts serious doubts on the success of the colonial and missionary enterprise.[4]

Africans are in no way regretting the benefits that have resulted from the encounter with modernity. Top on the list of such benefits are reading and writing, which carry the seeds of cultural continuity, development, and revolution. Christian missionary activity and the colonial machine were the chief vehicles of these benefits. In this study there is no agenda of a blanket condemnation of missionary work; nor is one even asserting that colonialism did not bring some sort of positive effect, even if it were "by default, by the iron law of unintended consequences" (Ali Mazrui).[5] But I like to emphasize that the present retracing of our steps back to the fundamental elements of our heritage is an affirmation that when these are modernized or updated, they will contain the indispensable seeds for the integral healing of Africans.

It is the thesis of this book that the retrieval and modernization of our African cultural matrix is the necessary route toward healing the political, economic, social and religious misery of Africa. The journey back to our roots must be made with a rigorous sociohistorical and comparative study. For the movement to endure and produce results that will transform the society, it must patiently search for the sociohistorical climate which favored the emergence, flowering, and eclipse of African societies and cultures. These dimensions of African societies and cultures—past and present—provide us with the material for philosophical and theological reflection.

African theology of inculturation considers the totality of African culture, ancient and modern, as the context of theology. Inculturation theology is first and foremost a reaffirmation of African culture and identity, denied by Western colonialism and Christian missionary evangelism. Thus it cannot escape from being called a theology of protest. Nor can it totally escape from the accusation of being an ethno-philosophy.[6] Second, it acknowledges that the message of Jesus the Christ, which must always be carried and communicated culturally, has come to dwell among us. Thus it is deeply connected with the idea of incarnation.[7] Third, the Jesus living among us in his community or church listens to new questions arising from the said community's reception of his message. And finally, the church (his body or the household of God) responds to this message, which has come to dwell among us, through her liturgy, spirituality, discipline, ethics, and theology.

The root of our problem is cultural. Consequently, to effect an enduring change, a radical cultural action becomes imperative. We are both the victims and agents of the negation of our fundamental cultural values, which are the resources we bring into our encounter with other groups of people and which may still constitute viable resources for the transformation of the continent. The uncritical imitation of the dominating Western culture—for example, in its cosmological and societal values—is responsible for the incoherence in our worship and social life. I like to emphasize, as many have tried to do, that one needs the African base to build a promising continent. Christians in Africa need the African base to construct a church which bears credible witness to the risen Jesus. This base must be founded on the retrieval of our fundamental cultural values. Africa must renew itself from its natural and sociohistorical resources. My reflections, which will center on the organization of the church in Africa, may thus fall generally within the theme of what is called the theology of inculturation. But while I shall employ elements of African social and religious organization in this reflection, I shall try to avoid being bogged down with the archaeology of African societies and religion. The ultimate aim of this cultural action is to liberate women and men in the continent from servitude.

African Theology of Inculturation

Inculturation is popularly described in Roman Catholic official and nonofficial documents as the incarnation of the Christian message in cultures. The idea of incarnation is derived from the Christian experience of the Incarnation of the Word. Thus one may continue the analogy for Africa by imagining the seed or sperm of the Christian message impregnating the fertile womb or land of Africa. The result is conception, pregnancy, and the birth of African Christianity. The message of Christ has become flesh. When this is said to happen within African cultures, it presupposes a type of marriage between the message of Christ and African cultures. Indeed some theologians and teachers of the church talk of marrying African values with Christianity. In African terms such an analogy of marriage calls up another analogy—covenant. Marriage involves a dialogue between two families, kindreds, or clans, which is concluded as a covenant or pact. Inculturation involves a dialogue between the whole way of life of Africans (especially the deepest level, where the crucial issues of life are faced) and the Christian message. The end product is an intimate bond between African cultures and the Christian message.

My interest is neither to define inculturation nor to put forward an idea of inculturation and indicate how it is already realized or may be realized in Africa. This in itself is an important task.[8] My chief interest is in designing a pattern of living Christian community in Africa that pays close attention to African sociopolitical and religious resources as well as to the Christian tradition. I would like to reexamine the kind of society which produced and produces African Christians—its patterns of organization and its potential for the renewal of our church and modern African societies. It is my belief that this society, taken in historical perspective, is the context for the emergence of a renewed African Christian community. If we have a crisis on our hands, how do we create the type of community or society which will show the way to its solution? As some say, how do we reconstruct? What kind of Christian community will ensure our autonomy (being free and dependent on our own resources) and our deliberate opening out toward other communities (communion)? In what kind of community do we hope to enjoy humane living in order to generate a humane culture? In other words, my interest is to contribute to the ongoing debate about the development of a relevant theology of the church which will display the Christian community as a credible agent of social transformation.

African Ecclesiology and Social Transformation

My overall interest enlarges the perspectives of the theology of inculturation to embrace issues of change, development, and liberation. The theology of a church-community that will become a credible witness to the social transformation of Africa is a theology which focuses on the emergence of an alternative society where the daughters and sons of Africa will enjoy their freedoms and liberties and participate in changing the continent. Today, there is an insistent call in the continent for the construction of the kind of society which will see Africa through its present crisis. For example, in Nigeria, a series of dialogues, conducted in the "Farm House" of Olusegun Obasanjo, on democracy led to the production of the book *Elements of Democracy.*[9] The discussions centered on the type of democracy suitable for Nigeria—a nation where an overpoliticized military has for decades eroded the basic elements of human rights, a nation where the majority of people are both poor and illiterate, a nation in which the traditional social institutions are still resilient, and, finally, a multinational, multireligious nation! The "Farm House" dialogue adopted the principle of democracy. But it also insisted on an African-styled democracy which takes on board dynamic African traditional values of democracy. Similarly, in their analysis and reflection on the sovereign national conferences, which swept through French-speaking Africa between 1989 and 1991, F. Eboussi Boulaga and Hubert Kamgang called for a reconstruction or a new beginning based on the retrieval and modernization of African values. The solution to Africa's problems is through mobilizing and ably harnessing its internal resources instead of depending on external aid.[10]

My interest in this study is to show that the development of a new way of being church in Africa will entrench in the Christian community the awareness that the church does not exist for herself. Her purpose is to bear witness to the risen Lord in the world. In Africa, this primary ministry will lead to the transformation of the continent and of the world. I shall show how the resources for this new evangelization are drawn from Africa.

The 1994 Special Assembly of the Synod of Bishops for Africa addressed a "Message to the People of God," in which the synod Fathers adopted a clear position on issues of justice, peace, and human rights. They underlined the relationship between peace and democratic rule. The bishops had severe things to say about tribalism, about responsible politics and the responsibility of the military in the spiral of violence cutting across Africa. They also acknowledged the many ways in which the church needs to reexamine herself, put her house in order, to bear witness to the gospel. In other words the church in Africa, during the synod, took responsibility to speak out against what she felt were conditions unfavorable for the enjoyment of full humanity by citizens of the continent.

This church, which sometimes speaks out and at other times appears less ready to take positions, is not a platonic institution. It is a local and localized community that may attract praise or blame for its role in the construction or reconstruction of Africa. It is a local church which is realized on many levels. But the most intensive context for the realization of the meaning of this church is the liturgical assembly in which the faithful are gathered to celebrate (especially the Eucharist) and "God's holy people, united in prayer . . . exercise a thorough and active participation at the very altar where the bishop presides in the company of his priests and other assistants."[11] It is a local church which, by taking or not taking a position on contextual issues, shows herself competent to assume her responsibility as the family of God, bearing witness by her life to the resurrection of Jesus. It is a church which enjoys her liberty and right as the People of God (assembly of the sons and daughters of God) and should not beg a sister church (e.g., Rome) for the liberties and rights which are constitutive of her very nature. This recognition of the resources of the church as an assembly which is a subject by right, with competencies deriving from her very origin or nature, is the starting point for assuming the mission of transforming the society (promoting democratization, justice, peace, and human rights in the church and society). She is the subject with a mandate to create an alternative society, the Kingdom which is to come being already present in her midst through her witness. The community speaks in a credible way and lives in truthfulness when it assumes with competence and dignity its liberties deriving from its internal resources.

The dependency syndrome and the search for external models are as much of a problem for the African state as for the church in Africa. This is why in this study I opt for a theology that arises from the resources of the living Christian community. The birth of the Christian community is the result of the encounter in history between traditional African societies and the Christian message. Consequently, African societies are the subject of the marriage with the Christian gospel. Impregnated with the seed of this gospel, renewed African Christian communities are born. The action taken by the communities to define themselves in the African world not only gives a personality to these communities but also affects the wider African world. African cultures are thus evangelized. Subjects, instead of objects of history, these communities organize their worship in assembly, live in mutual service, bear witness to the Lord in the world, and reflect on the life of faith in terms derived from the sources of their history. This experience produces a new way of being church. I would thus like to consider the emergent structures of an African ecclesiology as the point of departure for an African theology of inculturation. These structures will chart the way for bearing witness as Christians in the world and within the church community.

Division of the Study

The study begins with a brief survey of the African social organization in historical perspective. The survey starts with the modern period (chapter 2). In other words, it examines briefly the social order which was in place when Portuguese traders encountered Africans in the fifteenth century. It will point out the various patterns of organizing society and raise, as a point of interest, the African insistence on *sacred power,* or hierarchy; this insistence, curiously, prevents authority in the community from being absolute or autocratic. Traditional African societies are under the leadership of heads of families or kindreds or clans, and of chiefs or kings. First of all, these societies or communities are intimately linked with the sacred—humans and spirits interact in the social and political arena for the benefit of humans and the service of divinities. Religion and politics go together. Second, the society or community occupies a dominant position as subject. The interests of its survival (its life) override individual interests or rights. Indeed the community determines for individuals the range of their liberties, which are enjoyed only in the context of the community's vision of the world. Third, leadership is directed principally toward the realization of the well-being of the community—the living and the living-dead—as opposed to the selfish interests of leaders. And finally, the overriding ethical principle guiding the society is the promotion and protection of human life, which is of absolute value and which is the focus of all religious practice.

Furthermore, the study will show briefly how this social order was disrupted by slavery and colonialism. These two painful experiences introduced a different pattern of social organization and a new practice of religion. Authority was practiced in Africa by the victorious West as autocracy in both the political and religious spheres. The disruption of the social order ensured that the exercise of this autocracy turned African societies toward the interests of the superior power rather than be preoccupied with their internal needs. *Power* was exercised. *Sacred power* was experienced. But these became absolute, autocratic, and injurious to the well-being of society. The exercise of power was no longer directly linked to the interests of the African people because the social group no longer determined the direction of its life according to its interests and objectives. This *extroversion* of the life of the conquered societies affected all levels of life and did not diminish after political independence. This explains the persistent call for the political reconstruction of Africa. In the church it is a call for greater autonomy or inculturation (chapter 3). Its realization will give birth to a new way of being church.

This survey of our traditional social organization will lead me to merge or marry the original African vision—of constituting community and the exercise of authority within these communities—with the New Testament and patristic experience (chapters 4 and 5). The New Testament emphasizes the sovereign initiative of the Spirit of Jesus in the emergence of the church. The presence of the Spirit ensures the happy merging of communion and diversity within the church of Christ. For the patristic period particular attention will be paid to the North African church—especially to the ecclesiology of Cyprian of Carthage. This ecclesiology insists on the oneness of the church, the oneness of the priesthood manifested in the primacy of the See of Peter, and the autonomy of the North African church. The North African church had all the theological, legal, and disciplinary resources to live in harmony and to bear witness to the Christ in the world. The Roman church was not allowed to interfere in its internal affairs. The study will proceed to show how the original experience in our land, along with the resources of African tradition, elements of which still survived our turbulent history, form an integral part of the tools for the renewal of the Christian community in Africa.

The metaphor of *listening,* which appears in the title of this book, is drawn from the experience of the Manja of Central African Republic. The totem of the Manja chief is the rabbit because it has "large ears." The idea of listening, the study will show (in chapter 6), should inform and transform ministry in the church community; the emphasis will be on collaborative ministry. The metaphor of *listening* will also deeply modify the ministry of communion between the local churches and the primatial church of Rome.

CHAPTER 2

Traditional Institutions of Africa Encounter the West

I begin by making the surprising claim that many African traditional societies are democratically organized. While we may not delude ourselves that their structures are like those of modern democracies, I like to affirm that the fundamental elements of the democratic social organization in Africa need only to be updated or modernized for the realization of a dynamic process of democratization in contemporary Africa. Thus statements such as "Africa is not ripe for democracy" cannot be sustained after a patient study of African history and traditions. Second, the so-called democratization process which was started in French-speaking African countries in the 1990s does not necessarily represent a real experience of democracy. No doubt consultation with a people through the ballot box is an important element in the exercise of democratic rights; but this does not necessarily represent the full or adequate expression of democratic life as experienced in African communitarianism.

Democracy, informed by the communitarian experience of Africa, is a situation where people who make up a society are aware of their common interests and objectives, determine the way to realize such interests and objectives, and participate in the execution or realization of such aims and objectives of their society either directly or through their representatives. A government is thus democratic when members of the society are chosen or acclaimed to lead the society in the realization of its aims. Only a nation or society which negotiates in all sovereignty the conditions for its constitution into a nation and defines its aims and objectives may hope to live in democratic conditions. And similarly, only a church which assumes her autonomy and is responsible for her witness to the resurrected Jesus may hope to make a contribution to humane living in Africa. To argue these points, I shall examine the two principal ways of social organization in Africa before the modern period.

This chapter will provide a brief overview of the way societies were organized in Africa during the first significant contact between Africa and Europe in modern times. It will underline the worldview undergirding such societies and also describe the type of humans produced by these societies. It will then point out the consequences of the destabilization of African societies by the twin experiences of slavery and colonialism. The positive and negative roles of the Christian church in these two events will be highlighted. This introductory review prepares for the chapters that will argue for the reconstruction of African societies and church based on the resources of Africa.

The Organization of African Societies

The way a society functions is very important for the stranger. His or her security and the prosperity of his or her enterprise may depend on it. This is true in both prehistoric and modern times. Consequently, it is not surprising that traders, visitors, missionaries, and anthropologists from Western Europe always sought to know and be introduced to kings, chiefs, and heads of clans or families in those countries of Africa where they found themselves.

When the first Portuguese sailors and traders encountered the societies on the West coast of Africa in the fifteenth century, the period of modernity dawned for Africa. The isolation of the continent with its uninviting coastal lines came to an end. The Arabs who invaded the continent eight centuries earlier also ceased to be the principal link between sub-Saharan Africa and the Mediterranean world. The Portuguese had heard mythical tales of the incredible wealth (especially in gold and ivory) of West African kingdoms from their Arab informers. But there had been no direct contact between the two groups. The contact in the fifteenth century was thus the dawn of a new world. New possibilities could be opened from the contact. Merchandise and ideas could be exchanged for the mutual benefit of both communities. All in all, the break in the isolation of Africa, thanks to Portuguese technology and the enterprising Prince Henry the Navigator and his group, was an opportunity for Africa. The experience of slavery should not blind us to the need for such an encounter with other nations and systems for further development of Africa.

Historians and anthropologists acknowledge that the patterns of organizing society in place before the historic contact with the West defy easy classification. In other words it is not easy to identify these organizations with existing Western patterns of society. It will be impossible in this study to define the contours of each and every one of the varieties of organizing society in Africa. The hundreds of ethnic groups with differing practices and traditions make many wonder whether one should even talk about common elements in African social patterns. But I like to consider common features which emerge from African communitarianism, such as the typical African resources to be utilized in the reconstruction of African societies and church.

I follow some anthropologists in taking the risk of bringing together African patterns of social organization into two broad categories. There are, first of all, societies with dispersal of authority, or with authority in the hands of many. These are what some call "stateless societies" for the simple reason that they are not organized like the states as known to the West. Then there are those societies with centralized authority. These are the real "states" from the Western point of view.[1] While giving a brief outline of each model, I illustrate from representative societies. My selection of a particular sociocultural group may be arbitrary; but the choice tries to highlight patterns which derive from the resources of Africa and which I consider very useful for the reconstruction of our societies and church.

Authority in Many Hands

The idea of the exercise of authority by many leaders in relatively small communities appears to be the most common pattern of social organization in sub-Saharan Africa. This is the way followed by bands of hunters and gatherers such as the pygmies of Central Africa and the San of the Kalahari Desert. In principle these constitute small autonomous groups. There may not be more than a hundred people in the group. An elder or kindred head, assisted by or along with family heads, assumes ritual and political leadership.

This preference for the exercise of authority by many is also realized in fairly populous ethnic groups which are not receptive to a strong and centralized authority. An interesting example is the Igbo of Nigeria, who would be counted in the millions during the period under review. The most generalized pattern of social organization among them is the village-group. The village-group is a federation of clans. The clan is composed of kindreds, and the kindred made up of extended families. The head of the eldest or principal clan presides over the assemblies of the village-group attended by other heads. But decisions that affect the life of all the clans constituting the village-group necessarily involve consultation on family, kindred, and clan levels. Orders which come from the top without prior discussion or negotiation are ignored. The saying *igbo enweghi eze* (Igbo have no king) simply means that Igbo do not tolerate autocracy.

Each village-group is an autonomous community. Some constitute themselves into minikingdoms—like the Onitsha and West Niger Igbo, who have well-developed *Obi* (kings or chiefs) similar to the Yoruba or Bini experience. But these minikingdoms maintain the basic patterns of the Igbo experience of authority. In many communities aristocratic associations (*ozo*) may develop as a mark of success, with increasing political privilege and responsibility; also trade associations (medicine men, blacksmiths, etc.) and age grades are developed. It is a situation where laws or decisions affecting the society at various levels and in various shades and forms are discussed in meetings of the youth (age grades), married women, daughters (married to other village-groups), titled men and women, elders, *ofo*-holders (family, clan, or kindred heads), and so forth. Society is anchored on the sacred; and ritual is exercised on various levels by heads of families, kindreds, clans, and village-groups (ancestral cult, common festivals at the various levels, and related cults) and by priests of divinities (especially *Ala*—the Earth deity which, along with ancestors, presides over the land and its laws—in brief, over morality). Finally, there is a priest-kingship in one village-group (Nri). The king of this village-group exercises ritual authority in most of Igboland. He sends out priests from Nri to purify all manner of crimes or abominations committed against the land. Since there is no centralized authority, matters of litigation which are not resolved to the satisfaction of litigants may be referred to oracles, which are the last court of appeal. During the period of slavery, the *Ibini-ukpabe* oracle of the Arochukwu village-group was the most highly developed.

These societies, which prefer to entrust authority in many hands, are experienced with varying degrees of complexity by such ethnic groups as the Tiv of Nigeria and the Gikuyu of Kenya. In these societies there is an experience of what some have called republicanism or direct democracy. Contact with neighboring groups is facilitated by exogamy and trade. Disputes and wars necessitate treaties and agreements about safe passage of citizens of one group through another's territory. The power of these groups lies in persuasion rather than in coercion. There also lies their weakness. Their restricted numbers and limited range of coercive influence make them highly vulnerable. They may have a highly developed pattern of consultation, but they lack the force to defend themselves against a centralized and militant group. For example, in the thirteenth century, the Bini kingdom (founded by the Edo ethnic group) had little difficulty in overpowering Igbo village-groups. But the experience of centralized authority in the typical African pattern consists of a stronger federation of more groups.

Centralized Authority

The experience of centralized authority as found in African kingdoms has attracted more attention than the cases of dispersal of authority. These kingdoms are called "states" (according to the experience of the West) while the other types are classified as "stateless" societies. However, common elements undergird the formation of both types of society.

The primary characteristic of African kingdoms is the existence of a kingship—which is either hereditary (such as the Ganda) or elective (such as the Oyo, Yoruba). Second, these monarchies are either autocratic or oligarchic. Under autocratic or absolute monarchy, the ruler directly appoints and removes his representatives as he likes. This was the prevalent situation in those kingdoms, such as Mali and Songhai, which were under the influence of Arab-Moslem culture. The rulers (Mansa or Askia as they were called) appointed military commanders or slaves over provinces and districts, and these were directly responsible to the rulers. This kind of dictatorship is not characteristic of typical African kingdoms, though such a tendency remains a temptation to centralized authority.

The monarchies which are oligarchic are the more typical African pattern of kingship. There is a monarch, but the exercise of authority is collegial. It is a type of "constitutional monarchy." The Bini, Oyo, Egba, Hausa, Ashanti, Abomey, Zulu, Kongo, Swazi, and Ganda kingdoms are examples of such oligarchic monarchies (though the Hausa kingdoms were later influenced by Islamic culture after the Dan Fodio jihad and became centralized and autocratic).

The Yoruba kingdom of Oyo is a typical example. The Alafin is the head of the empire. His person is sacred. He is in intimate relationship with God and the divinities. Peace, justice, and prosperity are mediated to the kingdom through his person. To administer the immense Oyo territory, there are heads of districts, tribunals, the army, and so on. But working very closely with him on a daily basis is his council of chiefs—the Oyo-mesi (seven very powerful chiefs who meet twice a day to deliberate on the affairs of state). Indeed it is the Oyo-mesi which elects the Alafin. Each member advises the king on a key issue of state. The Bashorun (who is first among the seven) cross-checks the king's actions and can call for his removal. Next in rank are the army chiefs (eso—seventy captains who direct the wars that have been declared by the Alafin). The importance of the military increased during the slave trade. Then follow the clan chiefs and family heads. Since the Oyo empire was a confederation grouping together different units, heads of clans and families played an important role in the administration of the kingdom. There are also associations such as the Ogboni (more characteristic of the Egba kingdom) and the age grades (which in modern times have been assimilated into the association of youths—*egbe*).

The Oyo empire is a system in which a "divine king" assures order, peace, and prosperity; his authority is respected—he is said to have right over life and death; but the authority he exercises is collegial, with established principles to neutralize the monarch.[2]

The advantage of one monarch, as compared to the many heads in the clan and village-group organization, is cohesion, wider mixing of people, more efficient communication, faster realization of the objectives of state, more peace and prosperity, and so on. But our interest of course is not to point out which system is better than the other. Rather, it is to indicate the vision or resources of African societies in their social organization.

Common Traits in the Exercise of Authority

There are many common elements as well as differences in the African experience of the exercise of authority by many and of its exercise by a monarch. The difference between one king and many heads is clear, as our examples have shown. I shall highlight three common elements which are integral to the composition of these types of societies. I shall later show how important these elements could be in rekindling democracy in Africa and in renewing our interpretation of the way of being church.

First of all, there is a strong emphasis on *consultation and deliberation at many levels* in order to make decisions affecting the well-being of the society. Since the kingdom is a federation of clans or village-groups, the levels of consultation or deliberation experienced in the village-group or clan levels are reproduced in a more sophisticated way in the kingdom. But no level is omitted. In this way the opinion of the people governed is always expressed. One may correctly say that power lies with the people. The society or community is an active subject of right. It participates in decisions affecting its well-being. The deliberations have the general aim of arriving at a consensus. This is the famous African "palaver"—not to be understood as interminable and useless discussion; rather it is a system of mass consultation with the people. One could further illustrate this mass consultation in the symbol or totem of the Manja chief in Central African Republic. The chief's symbol is the rabbit, because it has large ears. He has the last word. But his ears are open to the opinion of all—humans as well as spirits. That is the source of his power; and that also is the limit of his power. Governance is delicate. The society is like an egg held in the hand. It must be protected from being broken.

Second, the *authority of rulers is respected*. This is a civic duty which is communicated through training, from the family to other established levels of socialization. The ruler is installed for the benefit of the community and ensures order, peace, and prosperity. The ruler is there to protect the interests of the people. The respect for his or her authority is linked to this indispensable service to the community. When he defaults in rendering this service either through moral failure or even sickness or old age, he is removed from office or killed. The gestures of respect vary from people to people—prostration, profound inclination, squatting while saluting, making way for the ruler to pass, and so on. Closely related to this respect for rulers is the respect for elders—parents, older brothers or sisters, older age grades, any older person, elders of the society, titled people. The summit of this respect for authority is the cult of ancestors among those ethnic groups where the cult exists.

Third, *authority is closely linked to the hierarchical conception of the universe*. The ancestors[3] are very close to God and the divinities. God's power and protection are described as enveloping human life; he is the sky in whose midst humans always find themselves without reaching, at any time, its periphery. God is the sun we cannot gaze at directly; he breaks iron as one breaks wood; he is the protector of all. Thus the ancestors who are closest to him mediate these powers and benefits to humans. The rulers or leaders of society are never chosen or acclaimed without the intervention or ritual presence of the ancestral spirits. Consequently, these rulers are very close to the ancestors. They are their representatives or even their emanations. In some communities this close association or identification of rulers with the power of ancestors leads to the ritual eating of a potent part of a deceased king or chief by his successor. Normally the heart of the chief is eaten! To respect authority is, indirectly, to respect ancestors and also God. Blessings follow such a civic duty, just as harm awaits the one who flouts the authority of the rulers. This is the sense in which authority is considered *sacred order* (*hieros archia*), or hierarchy. Interactions among humans are suffused with the presence of the sacred to ensure respect for lawfully constituted authority and freedom from abuse. The laws of society and the taboos surrounding people in authority prevent both anarchy and autocracy.

These elements show that Africa had the experience of a democratic order derived from its own resources, derived from its interaction with the environment. Athens may have taught the West the principles of democracy, but African communitarianism has contained these elements in African traditions as far back as memory can go. These need only to be modernized or updated to respond to the needs of Africa in the modern world. But if this is so, why is there such a great tendency today in Africa toward tyranny and the denial of democratic and humane living? Why did the nationalists, after independence, dismantle the structures of the Western-type democracy to transform what may be a legitimate leadership by one party into the dictatorship of a one-party state? Why are there so many military dictatorships? Why are the civil service and the apparatus of state negatively used against the development of humane living in most African countries?

It is here that we must underline the importance of recalling the experience of slavery and colonization and their impact on the African society and church. Unless such a radical recollection is attempted for healing, we shall never fully retrieve the fundamental values of the African experience of democracy.

Remembering Slavery and Colonization for Integral Healing

The point of departure for establishing justice, peace, human rights, and democratic or humane living in African society and church is a radical recollection of the African experience of slavery and colonization. This recalling can be negative or positive, creative or destructive. I prefer here the type of memorial which is creative. We do not remember in order to reproduce the hates, the violence, and the corruption which characterized our past. Rather we remember in order not to repeat such abominations and in order to transform such latent forces of domination into potent forces for the empowerment of the weak. Such an empowerment has as its aim the transformation of the universe.

Thus our recollection makes present the past in order to transform the future. It is radical because we shall not simply be interested in apportioning blame but shall be looking for the instruments for interpreting our own weakness and getting beyond such weakness. It is ritual because talking about evils or abominations committed in the past does not automatically wipe them away. The talking must become a ritual confession; from confession one must move to a plea for forgiveness; and forgiveness is expressed in a covenant where the God of the sky (who covers all) and of the land (who nourishes all) becomes our witness and sanctions such a ritual enterprise. In other words, the link between African communities, and the relationship between nations and continents, must not simply be based on declarations of principles (like the U.N. Declaration of Rights or the GATT agreement) but must be guided by ethical principles which must oblige all. I borrow this ethico-religious idea from the practice of making covenants (*igba ndu*—literally, binding lives together) among the Igbo and many other ethnic groups in Africa. There should be a principle beyond the contracting parties which will impose itself for the assurance of the honesty and truthfulness of the parties. This principle is God or any other agent of truthfulness. In international relations, the principle appears to be terror—as the Gulf War and other wars indicate. The memory of colonization and slavery will show us that such a reassuring principle has to be mediated in a nonviolent way. This will help us to establish in a later chapter the link between the prophetic witness of the church and nongovernmental organizations and the building of a peaceful world.

The Effects of Slavery and Colonialism

Slavery is a very ancient practice—as old as constituted kingdoms, as old as organized wars. Arab slave raiding and slave trading existed in Africa before the modern period. But European slave raiding and trading on the coasts of Africa have no comparison in the history of humankind. A recent study narrates from records of the raiders the trauma the victims underwent. And recent reflections on the issue lead to the conclusion that this crime against humanity should never be forgotten lest its continuing effects and the threat of its repetition be forgotten.[4]

Portugal was the leading slaving nation. Other European countries joined fervently, especially when they realized the benefits of the transatlantic trade. The Portuguese regime, like other regimes in Europe, was an absolute monarchy. The monarchy was supported by sacred authority—the sacred power of the church. For example, in his bull *Romanus Pontifex* (1454), Pope Nicholas V accorded to the king of Portugal a monopoly in trade and exploration along the west coast of Africa. The slaves who would be brought back from the Guinea coast would be baptized and won for Christ. Jurists, philosophers, and theologians, in those days, accepted the legality of black slavery as a matter of course. Even a great theologian and human rights-activist such as Bartolomé de Las Casas could be blinded for a time by the prevailing narrow thinking of sixteenth-century Europe to support black slavery. He made several requests (beginning in 1516) for the transportation of African slaves from Europe to South America to work the Spanish mines in order to free the Indians from slavery. Black slaves were regarded as more resistant human beasts of burden. Las Casas loved the Indians, whose humanity and liberty he ably defended. But the cause of the Africans did not initially enter his head. He later profoundly repented, before his death, of his error, realizing too late the weight his personality lent to the inhuman enterprise. When the enormity of his mistake dawned on him thirty years later, he did not lack the moral courage to denounce black slavery and to argue for the human rights of the blacks: "The blacks were enslaved unjustly, tyrannically, right from the start, exactly as the Indians had been."⁵

Two popes were later to condemn slavery (Urban VIII in his bull of April 22, 1639, and Gregory XVI in his letter *In Supremo* of 1839). However, the cooperation of the church in the crime against humanity and the theological justification which medieval Christianity gave to the enslavement of the black race have survived into the modern period. Indeed, during the First Vatican Council (1870), Daniel Comboni prayed the council Fathers to lift the curse on the children of Ham, a curse through which the Almighty had been punishing the sons and daughters of Africa with a cruelty unknown in the history of the human race.⁶ Mveng and others argue that no such curse was addressed against Africans; rather the Bible shows Yahweh taking the side of Moses and his Negro wife.⁷ But medieval Christian belief sustained such a curse, and the prayer for the conversion of Africa which was recited in many churches of Africa before Vatican II proves the continued presence of the belief. Half a millennium after the European invasion of the Americas (1992) John Paul II, during his visit to one of the principal African ports (Gorée, Senegal) where slaves were auctioned, called upon Africans to forgive the inhuman crime committed by those who called themselves Christians.⁸ One may forgive; but it will be an unpardonable crime to forget the causes of that human tragedy. It is a tragedy perpetuated by human beings who despised other human beings and whose quest for profit knew no limits.

Slavery and the Disorganization of African Societies

African societies along the coastal region were, first of all, disorganized and dislocated. For example, the Kongo kingdom, which was a confederation and whose king was killed in the battle of Mbwila or Ambuila (near the present Luanda, Angola) in 1665, broke into fragments. Second, Afro-Arab kingdoms concentrated on destabilizing villages and weaker kingdoms to increase the human merchandise. Huge armies were raised for self-defense and for slave-raiding. The Oyo kingdom had an army of about a hundred thousand men. New African slave kingdoms (like Opobo and Badagry in southern Nigeria) emerged or became strengthened to participate in the dehumanizing trade. Third, wars, raids, and disappearances of children, young men, and women became common not only on the coast but also in the hinterland. Interethnic or intertribal wars and wars between village-groups became more frequent. The channels of trade in salt, gold, leather, spices, and vegetables from North Africa down to the heart of the equatorial forest became solely channels of violence. Insecurity in civil society was the norm. Among the agricultural Igbo, parents going to farm normally hid their children in the ceilings of their homes.

One may never know the number of the victims of this trade. Between seven and fifteen million Africans may have been put on board slave ships for America. Half that number may have perished in dungeons. With the cream of the African youth wrenched from the continent, the economic, political, and cultural weakness of the continent became sealed. Finally, fear and distrust were implanted in the minds of Africans. Wealthy chiefs or kings may have sold their subjects, or were known to have sold their subjects, for European trinkets and gin. Thus the mentality came into existence that one person sells another to become rich, that one may use mystical powers (like witchcraft or sorcery) to steal children or to spirit people away to slave camps for slave labor to one's benefit.

The Crime of Our Ancestors

The participation of African kings, chiefs, and leaders of clans or village-groups in the obscene trade is very hard to understand. It is about the worst tragedy that has struck the continent. One may cope with being conquered, exploited, despised, and hated by other races. But when the worm is inside the bean the seed is destroyed with relative ease (as the Luba of Zaire would say). The value of values—human life—was devalued by many of our leaders. Many sons and daughters of Africa were denied their humanity and consigned to dungeons and concentration camps for slave labor. Values which were built for thousands of years were consigned to the dust-bin for European trinkets. Instead of the protector of the people, the leader became the enemy of the people. Instead of solidarity among members of a kingdom or a village-group, one sold one's kinsman for wealth. Instead of the law of hospitality, the stranger was unsure of his or her life. The practice became common to bury chiefs with a few heads. Human life, which the African vision of the world projected as the value to be protected, nurtured, and enhanced, was cheapened. Is it any surprise, then, that the confidence reposing on the king or chief as bringer of peace and prosperity was eroded in many coastal communities? Fear was implanted. Witchcraft became the imaginary device to balance the negative consequences of a society disorganized in its very structures of meaning. This dimension of our history must not be forgotten; it is a necessary ingredient for setting our house in order.

The shock of it all is what Africa exchanged for European goods during those four hundred years of trade. Dike has drawn attention to the fact that nothing of permanent value came to Africa during those four centuries. For example, in West Africa, in place of palm oil, ivory, gold, timber, and a superior labor force and other commodities which fed and buttressed European industries, Africa received the worst type of trade, "gin and meretricious articles."[9] Through criminal negligence, lack of foresight, and greed, our ancestors failed to learn the wicked intentions of the West. This failure or neglect is unpardonable. The assessment of Chinweizu is apposite:

> Four centuries, four long centuries wasted in particularist greed, four exhausting centuries bloodily exporting their kind, four centuries of political disorientation and social disorganization. May their souls sleep without rest in our memories to warn us away from any repetition of their ruinous neglect.[10]

Principles for Resisting the Violence of Slavery

But we must also note the resistance to this movement by some African societies and kingdoms. The Kongo kingdom was forced into a military option to defend the life of its citizens. King Alfonso I protested to the king of Portugal in 1526 that children of the nobility were being hunted by the Portuguese for enslavement. John III of Portugal replied in 1529 that slaves were the only merchandise the Kongo had for continued trade with civilized Europe. While the Kongo king may have tolerated and even participated in the trade of persons belonging to neighboring communities, he could not tolerate the practice of allowing his own people to be sold into slavery. When the Portuguese strengthened Luanda in the mid-seventeenth century as a base for raids and wars into the interior and gave the Kongo king Antonio impossible conditions, the king mobilized the whole society, raising an army of about one hundred thousand men for the disastrous battle of Mbwila. This is one pattern of resistance against slavery by many African societies to protect cherished values and traditions.

The example of the Nri village-group among the Igbo of Nigeria presents the strongest principled action against slavery and against the cheapening of human life in those difficult times. For the Nri, and the Igbo in general, human life is sacred, an absolute value. Any attempt on human life, even accidentally, must be purified. In some Igbo village-groups the penalty for the accidental killing of a human person is seven years of exile and the destruction of the property of the culprit. Consequently, during the period of slavery slaves were neither bought nor sold in Nri markets nor in the markets of Nri colonies. To practice such a trade in Nri markets would be an abomination. Furthermore, the Nri considered any war an evil because it involved the shedding of human blood. According to Nri sacred narrative such bloodletting would pollute the earth and violate the covenant between God and humans:

> Thus there was a covenant between earth and man. . . . No person should defile the earth by spilling human blood in violence on it. This is the covenant. It must be kept. We Nri keep it. We told other Igbo to whom we gave yam to keep it.

Rather than be involved in violent activities, the priest-king of Nri, who presides over the priestly village-group, sent priests all over Igboland to persuade people to live in peace and to purify the earth polluted by violence. Throughout the turbulent period of slavery and colonization, it is on record that only once in Nri history did an Nri king take up arms to fight a war. The aim of the war was to resist the Abam mercenaries who were hunting for slaves for the Aro group. An Nri historian, however, called the action of the king "a mushroom attempt," for, after all, "it is an abomination to kill any human being even in war."[11]

Slavery was so devastating to Igbo society and culture that the very precincts of the sacred were not spared. The Ibiniukpabe oracle of Arochukwu was exploited by the Aro Igbo for slavery. Among the Igbo the oracle is the last court of appeal. When an accused person is convicted by Ibiniukpabe, he or she is said to have been "eaten by Chukwu" (God). Since the oracle was highly frequented thanks to the Aro propaganda and the increased distress of the time, many people were thus "eaten by Chukwu" and sold into slavery. The Aro went further to employ Abam mercenaries (from another village-group) to fight their wars in order to capture slaves. Fear and distrust of the Aro Igbo persist to the present day. It is here that the virtue of the Nri village-group, organized around a priest-king, in totally rejecting violence and the shedding of human blood must be recognized. Their role and history among the Igbo remain a paradigm for the renewal of Igbo society and even for the reconstruction of African societies.

Nri civilization does not tolerate holy wars, crusades, or jihads. This is a society where religion is at the service of humane living. Today more than ever such humane living eludes Nigeria, Africa, and the world. Our societies need to be reconstructed on the sound ethical principle that any attack on human life sends out shock waves of disorder on the earth. It is an offence against the earth, against the owner of the earth, and against the inhabitants of the earth.

African Religiosity and Integral Humane Living

Sometimes one hears that religion has become a disease in Africa, that religion is an obstacle to the development of the continent. Some allege that right from the time of slavery to our own day, the African religious vision of the world substitutes escapism for facing the social, political, and economic challenges of the continent. The enslaved blacks in America developed the Negro spirituals as a means of carrying their burden without being liberated from it, without even knowing that heavy hands were unjustifiably laid on them. The poor in Africa pour into independent churches, healing homes, sects, and charismatic groups and delight in highly emotional or culturalist liturgies in order to drown their pains in the irrational/emotional instead of questioning the very structures which produce such pain or oppression. The fatalism which is part of some patterns of African traditional religion and culture appears to be encouraged by this pattern of religious practice in times of crisis—past and present.[12]

There is no doubt that sometimes religion may provide an escape route for the suffering poor; that sometimes religion may be exploited by priestcraft to direct the sufferers away from the real causes of their suffering; that sometimes it may represent the ineffective cry of the oppressed, the soul of a soulless condition, the opium of the poor. It is true also that there may be a tendency among many pastors of the black church in America to talk about "heaven over yonder" instead of a direct involvement in the affairs of this world to change it. Some pastors from all denominations in Africa or America may stress the emotional at the expense of the rational for reasons varying from formation, personal limitation, or love for money to a distrust of the intellectual or a preference for not being involved in a demanding social analysis. But to interpret the Negro spiritual as an example of escapism is to be ignorant of the power of this corporate composition to give cultural identity to the brutalized slaves. Some more nuanced interpretations show that the constant refrain of being "free at last" and the reference to "heaven" in the spirituals are not totally symptomatic of withdrawal from this earth to a place of rest. They also symbolize taking the train from the southern states, where slavery was the rule, to the northern states, where slavery had been abolished. But even if the spirituals, which are very much in touch with the culture of the oppressed, embody otherworldly sentiments, they represent clearly the limit of the power of the slave master. He may have power over the body of the slave, which can be beaten to submission, but power over the person or "soul" of the slave eludes him. For according to the psalmist, power ultimately belongs to God (Ps 62:2-5).

The spirituals laid the foundations of the struggle for the civil rights of the blacks in America. It is part of the product of the black church, which bestowed on black Americans "a somebodyness that racism could not destroy." According to James Cone, the firm faith expressed in the spirituality of the black church that "God did not bring us this far to leave us," along with the preference for Old Testament models of justice and liberation, constituted the elements which created the "justice, love and hope" themes of Martin Luther King's struggle for civil liberties. King criticized in no uncertain terms the otherworldly preaching of many black pastors. But it was the spirituality of black religion that enabled blacks to know that they were human beings. This originated from their African culture and was forged in the struggle to make sense of their lives in a nation of white so-called Christians. This spirituality created Martin King and his like.[13]

The political and liberation ring of popular religiosity in Africa has been maintained from the time of the emergence of independent churches. Being a product of the social, political, economic, and religious revolutions in colonial Africa, they cannot be excluded with a wave of the hand as simply the emergence of the irrational; they fully form part of the solution to these problems. Some of these churches separated from the parent missionary churches either because of the racialist discriminatory policies of the missionaries or because of the insufficient attention paid to the African spiritual, human, and cultural values. It is instructive that about half of the six thousand such churches which emerged in Africa are found in South Africa alone. To interpret these movements as the irruption of the irrational is, to say the least, naive.

To illustrate the close relationship between religious practice in Africa and liberation movements, I shall describe one of the oldest religious movements in the old Kongo kingdom. This movement combined both politics and culture with a new kind of Christianity in the late seventeenth and early eighteenth centuries. This is generally called the Antonine Movement. It was led by a young lady of singular character, Kimpa Vita, better known as Dona Beatrice and popularly acclaimed by her followers as St. Anthony. In brief, the Portuguese destroyed the Kongo army and disorganized the kingdom after the battle of Mbwila. The capital of the kingdom (San Salvador—Mbanza-kongo) was deserted and overgrown with weeds. The various clan chiefs or kings who made up the federated kingdom were at war with one another. No clear leader emerged to unify the kingdom. Dona Beatrice emerged with the singular purpose of uniting politically the split kingdom through the spiritual support of a Catholicism cut to the measure of the Kongolese religious universe. She confronted a Portuguese Capuchin, Father Bernardo da Gallo, and wanted to know why there were no African saints. An older woman, Fumaria, had been announcing visions of the apocalyptic destruction of the people if the king did not come down from the hills to resettle in and rehabilitate the capital, San Salvador. People were calling Fumaria a saint. Dona Beatrice connected the recognition of African saints with the political unity of the kingdom. Her verbal outburst before Gallo, who was later to condemn her to be burnt at the stake, was significant.

> You do not want to recognize Congo saints. That explains why you want to lay hold of the old woman [Fumaria] and chastise her. You do not want the restoration of the kingdom. You do not have sufficient courage to do it as she will do it.[14]

She was able, through her negotiations, to bring the warring chiefs under one united kingdom, though the chief she favored did not save her from the stake on the July 1, 1706. But her movement was able to re-create the Christian symbols in terms of the Kongo experience: Jesus Christ was born in San Salvador, which then became Bethlehem, and he was baptized in Nsundi, or Nazareth. The favorite Christian saints were Kongolese by origin. St. Anthony, known for his intercession in hopeless cases, was identified with the leader of the revolution, and St. Francis, admired for his poverty, was also made a Kongolese in this radical transformation of Christian religion into an African religion. Even after her execution Dona Beatrice was reputed to die and rise every week and to bestow fecundity to women. And her cult and following have continued. This is religion at the service of the political unity and cultural identity of a people. One may criticize the accuracy of the theological interpretation of the movement, but one may hardly fault it in terms of the commitment of a people to their liberation.

These and other movements demonstrate that Christian religious practice in Africa has the potential for participating fully in the integral human development and liberation of the suffering peoples of Africa. I am not saying that theologies and liturgies which emphasize identity and culture, emotion, and dependence on the intervention of heaven, are not prone to errors and exaggerations. But I like to insist that their original vision forms part of the contribution of religion in the struggle to free a colonized people from the yoke of oppression.

Colonialism and the Turning Away of Africa

The colonial ideology is that of domination and exploitation of the colonized, intended to derive maximum profit from minimum investment. To realize this objective, the colonizers went ahead to deny the being of the colonized, their person, their culture, their worldview. In its place was installed the person, the culture, and the universe of the colonizer for the realization of the interests of the latter. The successful implementation of this ideology alienated the colonized.

The machine for the realization of the colonial ideology was both technical (colonial military superiority) and religious (Christianity). Even if some missionaries opposed the methods of the colonizers, evangelization and colonization were linked; this link was even foreseen in the Berlin conference of 1884-1885, where Africa was partitioned. Consequently, the conquering Western powers set out to colonize, that is, to occupy lands which did not belong to them, and to impose forced labor on populations to extend their domination and to develop their home economies. They also set out to civilize Africans: schools were introduced, and these were administered principally by missionaries; new technologies were installed; a new culture was born. And, finally, they Christianized Africa: Western Christian cosmology and notions of person and community were introduced to compete with or displace the local African cosmologies. This close link between the Christian religion and the political powers in the conquest of Africa must not be forgotten in the struggle for the reconstruction of the continent.

The Radical Subjugation and Exploitation of Africa

The consequences of the colonial experience were enormous. First, the societies which had been weakened through slavery were either totally destroyed or subjugated. Every member of the society was reduced to the level of the masses, including the chiefs and rulers. The local hierarchy was replaced by an administrator representing a foreign autocratic regime. Chiefs or communities which allied with one colonial power or the other, or concluded treaties for their own interest or advantage, discovered too late the intent of the colonial ideology—total subjugation for the interests of the colonizer. One may compare this situation to the sixteenth-century Kongo kingdom where the king invited the Portuguese to establish schools in his court and he became one of the students. The modernization at that time was not to the detriment of the local hierarchy but was under its control. The sacred institution which supported the colonial domination was the Christian church, which never condemned colonialism as it did, with time, condemn slavery.

Second, the subjugated kings or chiefs and the nobodies installed as chiefs (for example, among the Igbo) lost favor with the local population and even became despicable in their eyes. They had to mobilize the population for forced labor; and oftentimes labor was not drawn from their own kindred. Many who were displaced from their homes to labor camps (for example, in the Ivory Coast and Cameroon) never returned. Witchcraft and sorcery became more entrenched as imaginary devices to interpret the action of these rulers who could spirit people away into labor camps.[15]

Third, a new class of Africans started to emerge. These were indigenes who participated in the new administration or those who were preparing themselves to take over from the colonial administration.

Fourth, all orders were received from the outside at all levels. African societies became restructured to respond only to external stimuli. This situation of extroversion was operative in both the secular and the sacred domains. Cash crops such as groundnuts, cotton, cocoa, and coffee and mineral products such as coal and tin were produced or extracted for the colonial industries of the West. No such industries were established in the colonies. The cultivation of food crops such as millet, rice, and tubers for local consumption and the upgrading of traditional metallurgy and local weaving industries were discouraged. These products had to be imported through the medium of the colonial masters. Africans forgot the art of gold, tin, iron, and copper mining and smelting and the working of related products. Consequently, the African peoples lost control of the politics and economy of their continent to the predators. They were no longer the originators of their own designs, nor were they the projectors of their own schemes or the creators of the events that led to their destiny.[16] Work, insofar as it was public, insofar as it was related to government, became vitiated. It was done for the interests of predators. It was not public service for the well-being of society so one could cheat. Civil service and the whole apparatus of state began with this inherent lie. In the church, Latin rituals or rituals of other churches were indiscriminately introduced with their patterns of initiation and they were all closely linked to the school system, while the native rituals of initiation were not only discouraged but were declared diabolic. The highest virtue for being selected as a minister in the church (priest or bishop) was the readiness to obey and the openness to be schooled to comply with orders coming from outside. Finally, Africans became primitive, savages, infants, lazy, at all levels. This is how Africa was invented—the famous anthropological impoverishment of Africa.[17]

The Colonial Invention of the African Primitive Native

It then became normal to apply Darwinian evolutionary theories in the study of societies. A. Comte's law of three hierarchical levels formed the background for some anthropological studies of colonized societies as a strategy to justify their subjugation and exploitation. Each society passes from magic through religion to science, from promiscuity through a matrilineal to a patrilineal family system, from savagery through barbarism to civilization.[18] Colonizers, anthropologists, and missionaries shared this climate of opinion. Thus, Samuel Baker could say that none of the races of the Nile basin had any knowledge of the supernatural or the supreme being, not even any superstition. Their spirits were as stagnant as the stagnant water around them. Or according to Richard Burton, studying African religion gives one the feeling of adults observing children at play.[19] Thus colonization, from the anthropological point of view, was the best thing that could have happened to Africa.

From our study of the organization of African societies it is clear that such remarks lack historical accuracy. They are, rather, a justification for the continued exploitation of and discrimination against the conquered Africans. If one consulted Greek historians such as Herodotus (sixth century B.C.E.) or Diodorus of Sicily (first century C.E.), one would hear that Africa (the Nubian region normally called Ethiopia) was the cradle of civilization and religion. Both historians referred to the well-known passages of Homer's *Iliad* to show how Jupiter led the other divinities every summer into Africa to receive their sacrifices.[20] Those who visited Egypt after the Napoleonic conquest (end of the eighteenth and beginning of the nineteenth centuries) testified to a different manner of classifying the human race in ancient Egypt. Analyzing the bas-relief of the tomb of Ousirei I, sixteenth century B.C.E., Champollion-le-Jeune in his thirteenth letter to his brother noted how the Egyptians classified humanity in a hierarchical order. First, the inhabitants of Egypt, followed by black Africans, then Asians, and the last and least in the series, Europeans.[21] Such historical records, however, are interesting neither for the colonial ideology nor for the aims of Christian missions. Africans should thus disregard such biased writings in the present task of cultural, religious, political, and economic reconstruction. The basis of this reconstruction is the immense human and natural resources and the values undergirding the African societies in their historical perspective.

The Ethics of Reconstructing Colonized African Societies

The violence which accompanied colonization and evangelization has to be rejected in the reconstruction of the continent. The collusion of the churches with the colonial aims and objectives shows what can still happen if the churches do not keep their distance from any type of regime in order to confront whatever challenges the society faces. The reactions of the mass of Africans and the elite on the cultural, political, and military levels either to fight against or collude with colonization and the discrimination against Africans have to be assessed and assumed by Africans in both their negative and positive dimensions. But, for the reconstruction of Africa, the realism of the global village must not escape us. The issue of the reconciliation of Africa with the powers which enslaved and colonized her should be courageously faced. Reconciliation presupposes the admission of guilt. In our present situation of weakness, dependency, and misery, we attract at best the pity of our former tormentors, and at worst their scorn. We should initiate the great dream or be part of it in order to reestablish the fundamental value of human life and humane living as the ethical basis of reconstruction.

The ethics of reconstruction will not be based on the violence and brutality of those who conquered us or who were victorious without being righteous. The memory of our past is not a negative recollection. The realism of the world economic, political, and military orders does not even allow us to pursue the path of vengeance. Reconstruction may not be based on antagonism but on reconciliation. To midwife such a reconciliation in an interdependent world, the ministry of a nonviolent and nonpartisan organization is necessary for Africa and the world. Such an organization mobilizes all concerned persons to act against all manner of oppression of the human person. This body must be nongovernmental, in order to guard against the excesses of governments. It must be international or intercontinental, because in the global village actions performed at one end of the globe affect others. It must be nonviolent in its choice of means to realize objectives, in order to show that the supreme value is the life of each and all. An Nri political theologian (Nwaokoye Odenigbo) enunciated the ethics of this new order in his criticism of colonialism and slavery:

> When the white men came, they asked us to abrogate the codes of abomination and taboos. They said that they had brought peace based on different ideas. We agreed and decided to watch them. Today, we see war everywhere; we see brothers have sex with their sisters, we see people strangulate others to acquire their wealth. The white men brought many good things; they brought

peace between Igbo communities but they have not brought peace within the communities. We Nri brought peace within communities when we ruled. We are doing all we can to bring peace between communities but the slave trade did not allow us to, and the white men came and stopped us from ruling. White men have arms and we do not believe in fighting. Fighting spills blood on the earth and this is an abomination. The white men that came started by killing those who did not agree with their rules. We Nri never did so: we tried to persuade and convince people not to do so. Okoli Ijeoma of Ndikelionwu and the Edo did what the white men did—they killed people. We Nri condemn it.[22]

Condemnation of such acts of violence is only a first act. The building of viable communities which will supervise the reign of ethics in international relations is the necessary basis for peace. The Christian church, in fidelity to the vision of its founder, may make a significant contribution to realizing such a utopia. Many church groups and episcopal conferences in Africa and the world have joined voices in condemning the violence in the politics and economy of the world today. But a more viable pattern of life must first be shown to be possible to lead the society out of the present confusion. It is in this way that a new way of being church in Africa and in the Christian world may start the transformation of Africa and the whole planet earth from the inside.

CHAPTER 3

The Reconstruction of African Societies and Church on the Principles of Democracy and Human Rights

In 1991 the All Africa Conference of Churches (AACC) adopted an action program to enable the churches to make their contribution to the reconstruction of Africa. This is what it called the theology of reconstruction. It is a theology which will help African societies to resolve creatively the present crisis. In my view this theological program can only be realized on the basis of assembling and updating or reinterpreting the human and natural resources of Africa in terms of the Christian gospel. Again in my view such a theology of reconstruction should not be limited to outlining ethical imperatives for civil society. Like Jesus who began to do and to teach, the Christian church may bear a convincing witness to the gospel by applying and living out such ethical principles within her communities.[1]

My views on this reconstruction are summarized under two headings: (a) the relational notion of the human person should control the exercise of democratic and human rights, and (b) the full respect of rights and freedoms within the local and universal church is the highest testimony of the transformation of human societies. I shall briefly treat the issue of the relational notion of person in the present chapter and then consider the question of rights and freedoms in the church in chapter 4.

The Relational Notion of Person and Human Rights

The principles which I have described above as undergirding African democratic institutions indicate a system of social control based

35

on channels of relationship. From small-scale communities to the more complex kingdoms, the social organization is based on a complex of relationships and survives by servicing such relationships.

In most African societies the individual human is described in terms of a complexity of relationship. Since Africa is varied, various anthropologies of the person must thus exist. But in the West African subregion, and among some ethnic groups of Cameroon (such as the Bamileke), a lot of similarity and even identity exists in the conception of the human person.

The most common characteristic of the way humans living in West African societies are conceived is "relatedness." Among the Igbo it is impossible to define the characteristics of a person without linking him or her to parents and departed ancestors "reincarnate" in the person. Many West African societies have sacred narratives (myths) about the preexistence of each human as spirit in the land of the dead. Each person incarnates into the human world through the creative act of a protective (dynamic) spirit assigned to the person by God. The spirit is known by various names in West Africa—*chi* (Igbo), *ori* (Yoruba), *kra* or *okra* (Ewe, Asante), *ka* (ancient Egypt).

In addition to the above links, the human person could be expressed as a multiplicity of souls or life principles. For example, the Bambara of Mali have eight such principles which are paired. Among the Asante (Ghana) the elements which compose a person can be reduced to seven. Sarpong summarized these elements in a recent paper.[2] In the first place, there is *mogya* (or blood, the base of the clan system in a matrilineal society; this matrilineal part of the person dies). Then there is *okra* (the part of the person which does not die). The *okra* is not reducible to the soul, since it has a cult. It is rather the guardian spirit, the humanizing part of the person. There is the *sunsum*. This is a spiritual preexistent principle. It is changeable. It can be trained to be "heavy" instead of being "light." As a "featherweight" the *sunsum* can easily fall prey to the action of witches. It is the individualizing principle in the human person. Then there is the *sasa*, which Sarpong describes as the avenging part of the human person; it incites a wrongdoer to confess wrongs committed against others. The *ntoro* is a spiritual element transmitted by the father which calls for the respect of one's father. After puberty one is guided by one's personal *ntoro*. Finally, there is the *saman,* which is the form a person assumes after death.

These elements are constitutive of the human person. Relationship is not simply a way in which the subject may realize itself. It is the essential element of "personhood." The quality of a person is dependent on the intensity of maintaining these relationships.

One may thus appreciate the importance of initiation and passage rites in the growth and development of persons in Africa. Through these rites one learns about and experiences the channels of relationship in order to become a person. One is human because of others, with others, and for others (*motho ke motho ka batho ka bang*[3]—a Sotho, South African, proverb): "I am because we are, and since we are therefore I am." "I belong, therefore I am." The tension toward (motion) is a constitutive dimension in the emergence of the human person.

This notion of person in West Africa is opposed to the classical Greek notion of *stasis*, which considers motion or change as accidental and as an imperfection. Systems biology insists that an organism is a living organism when all the interconnections which make it up are active. Death results when these connections break down. Among humans, these interconnections provide the essential components for the social definition of the person. Similar interconnections constitute the basis for the emergence and survival of a small-scale community, a kingdom, or a nation. This idea of relatedness underlies Martin Luther King's "Dream" for a free nonracial America. He may not have known that he was drawing from the universal (African) definition of the human person when he asserted in that famous speech of 1961, "Strangely enough, I can never be what I ought to be until you are what you ought to be. You can never be what you ought to be until I am what I ought to be."[4]

Some believe and fear that since these interconnections operate in kindred or tribal settings, they are unusable and are even destructive in the modern multiethnic or multinational states. Group solidarity, along with other moral imperatives, tends to limit its operation within the ethnic group or within kindreds and clans which can trace their origin to an ancestor—real or putative. The conflicts in Rwanda/ Burundi (where the BaHutu are pitched against the BaTutsi, leading to barbaric massacres) and Ghana/Togo (where the Kokumba are fighting against the Namumba) are sufficient contemporary examples to warn against the archaic African models of social organization. Indeed the saying that "blood" links are thicker than "baptismal water" became part of this pessimistic assessment of African systems of social organization during the 1994 Synod for Africa in reference to the Rwandan massacres, where Christians savagely butchered fellow Christians.

Building Relationships beyond Ethnic Groups and Races

African societies are not inexperienced in federating nations, as the history of African kingdoms shows. Solidarity within the ethnic group and between groups is not built on a lie but on truth and is linked to control by spiritual forces. The conflicts which began during the slave trade and matured at the colonial period gave birth to the lie which we call African states with their artificial boundaries. This lie created the dominant extroversion of the societies, making them respond simply to the interests and objectives of the colonizers. At independence the nationalists were unable to get beyond this lie. Only leaders such as Kwame Nkrumah saw through the lie and called for the political unity of African societies.

The challenge of reexamining the meaning of solidarity in modern Africa must be courageously faced. Indeed, a new, viable, and dynamic model for building relationships beyond the limits of ethnicity has become imperative. In order to achieve this, it is my view that the interests and objectives of the ethnic groups, nationalities, and communities which make up Africa must be creatively received and reinterpreted as constitutive elements for the reconstruction of Africa. These interests and objectives will, in turn, be creatively harmonized with the reality of modern Western patterns, adopted since independence, which have become part and parcel of the African heritage, so that viable nations, regions, and a united Africa will emerge.

In the first place, I like to insist that in the precolonial past, the interests and objectives of ethnic groups assured the servicing and safety of the trade routes, for example, in the West African region, across the Sahara, and through the equatorial forest. Salt, gold, leather, spices, copper, and vegetables were exchanged with relative ease along these regions before the same routes were converted into slave routes. Warring communities adopted realistic patterns for creating channels of solidarity to protect their economic and political interests. Marriage was the commonest way of binding feuding communities together in order to limit violence.

At the dawn of the colonization of southern Nigeria, the Onitsha Igbo wanted to protect their economic, cultural, and religious interests and to negotiate on terms of equality with the missionaries and their British trading partners (the West African Company), whose trading terms and trade monopoly were against the best interests of the Onitsha community. At a meeting organized between the Onitsha chiefs and Bishop Adjai Crowther, the head of the Church Missionary Society mission, the chiefs made their interests and objectives clear: the missionaries should change their style or quit bag and baggage; missionary preaching was doing harm to traditional practices and loyalties; they should stop introducing an alien lifestyle, such as giving T-shirts to their members, because it was creating a social dichotomy; the bishop should intervene with the West African Company in favor of the Onitsha community for better trade terms. However, to ensure prolonged cooperation with the immigrants and to protect the benefits accruing from the relationship, the chiefs proposed to seal the relationship with a marriage pact. According to Crowther, the chiefs demanded "that an agreement should be entered into for intermarriage between the children of the settlers and those of the natives of Onitsha that all may become one people, or else they could not see how we could profess to be their friends without such arrangement."[5]

Bishop Crowther, who was asked to negotiate the pact, was not receptive to the Onitsha wisdom. The Onitsha chiefs were convinced that the sealing of such a relationship with marriage pacts would ensure the elimination of violent or inimical acts from one or the other. When Crowther turned down all their requests, the chiefs decreed a boycott of the missionaries. The relationship deteriorated. Between 1868 and 1880 living together became very tense. British trading interests became more intolerant of competition (especially from the French). The militarily weaker Onitsha community was on the receiving end of unfair trade relations and missionary propaganda. Finally, on October 28, 1879, after British citizens had been carefully evacuated, Onitsha was brutally bombarded by a British gunboat. A similar bombardment took place in 1880.[6] Such gunboat diplomacy as witnessed in Onitsha was popularly known in the British colonial dictionary as "pacification."

From the resources of African political experience, marriage was a very powerful means of creating new solidarities (cf. King Solomon of the Hebrew Scriptures). In addition to kinship ties through marriage, most African societies have blood-pact rituals to seal new relationships which are generally as intimate and as demanding in solidarity as family or clan relationships. The blood-pacts can be sealed among friends, lovers, and cult groups. They could create relationships and fraternities that go beyond ethnic groups, such as the blood-pact ritual of the Lyangombe cult, common among ethnic groups in Zaire, Rwanda, Burundi, and Uganda.[7] Common experiences of oppression cutting across ethnic groups established transethnic bonds during the era of colonialism. For example, one of the strongest resistance movements against colonial rule in East Africa, the Majï Majï movement, was transethnic. Under the oppressive hands of the German colonizers, peasants from more than twenty ethnic groups rose up against exploitative German labor policy. The unsuccessful movement had as its religious base the religion of the ancestors.[8]

These transethnic links, which are part and parcel of the African experience of person and political organization, are necessary tools for reexamining the tribalism or ethnocentrism that accompany the African systems of social organization especially as they have evolved in the postcolonial period.

If we admit, from the review of our past, that African societies must be rebuilt on the basic interests and objectives of the various nations and peoples which make up Africa, we must equally admit that these interests have to be critically and judiciously reviewed to avoid the weaknesses of tribalism and ethnocentrism, which are there for all to see. We may not only adapt the modern Western democratic structures to our traditional patterns of social organization but also adopt the advantage which became easier during the colonial times— of mobility for all, irrespective of rank or class, from one ethnic group to another. This offsets the disadvantage of the artificial colonial boundaries. Also we adopt the advantage of the modern democratic systems of government to overcome the limitations of governance within ethnic nationalities.

It must be repeated over and over again, there is nothing sacrosanct about the colonial boundaries despite the resolutions of the Organization of African Unity. The misgovernance which bedevils Africa and the facility with which African rulers employ violence (the police, the military, and the presidential guard) to stay in power tell about whose interests are being protected in African nations. The gross denial of the basic rights of citizens by military dictators and dictatorships of one-party states show the nonviability of the states as they exist today. The terms for the union have to be renegotiated. The interests of the nations making up each region have to be respected, and the principal objective of these renegotiations would be the political unity of Africa.

It is against the interests of Africans to continue maintaining what Hubert Kamgang rightly calls the more than fifty "lilliputian states" whose dictators keep on terrorizing the sons and daughters of the continent. Africa must unite.[9] A new wave of social-psychological, political, and economic education has to be introduced to teach our young people the historical roots of the links between Africans, the necessity of maintaining and intensifying such links in the global village, the anthropological basis of living in relationship, and the obligation of getting out of the narrow vision of the "nation-prison" for the construction of one African nation. Thus one is led to see one's rights and privileges interconnected with the rights and privileges of all children, youths, women, and men of Africa in order to participate with dignity in the reconstruction of the world at large. A body such as the Christian church, which lives this unity in freedom within its own circle, may be very well equipped to engage in the prophetic and educational mission of the reconstruction of Africa.

Human Rights Guided by the African Relational Notion of Person

It is on the basis of the relational notion of the person and the aims and objectives of nations and communities that make up Africa that one should defend the creative enjoyment of democracy and human rights. When Western governments and nongovernmental organizations such as Amnesty International, Human Rights Watch, or Africa Watch talk about human rights, they speak from a notion of the free individual person who must remain unfettered to act, speak, worship, associate, or accumulate wealth. Thus, when Ken Saro-Wiwa, the Ogoni (Nigerian) poet and fighter for the rights of his people, is imprisoned, Western governments and human rights groups cry foul. And the Nigerian military junta, in order to continue doing business with the West, makes the gesture of abiding by the rule of law and protecting the rights of individuals by freeing Ken. This is the predictable behavior pattern of military dictatorships in Nigeria. However, early

November 1995, the Sanni Abacha junta introduced a new twist into the barbarism of Nigerian dictatorships by the judicial murder of Saro-Wiwa and eight other Ogoni activists. Nigeria, Africa, and the world were shocked. Pressures were mounted to bend the military cabal. The fact that African dictators sometimes bow to such pressures and agree to free activists or dissidents in itself is a victory for the humane treatment of individuals. It is reaping the benefits for all humanity of the fruits of the struggle against arbitrary dictatorships and the rule of divine kings. The Americans won this right through the Bill of Rights of December 15, 1791; the French Revolution inscribed it in the *Déclaration des Droits de l'Homme et du Citoyen* of August 26, 1789; and the United Nations organization enshrined it in the Universal Declaration of Human Rights of 1948. African countries are signatories to this U.N. declaration. Furthermore, they are signatories to the African Charter for Human and Peoples' Rights of 1981. In the present struggle to rid Africa of inhuman dictators, churches and human rights groups should rely upon these signed declarations to denounce oppression in order to reduce the suffering of the persecuted.

Beyond Modern Western Individualism

But this struggle for rights on the level of the individual is insufficient. The tradition on which this definition of rights is based relies heavily on the modern Western individualistic notion of person. True enough, classical Greek philosophy and Roman juridical culture preferred the static or ontic definition of person. The core of the classical Greek tradition was passed on to medieval Christian thinkers through Boethius, who defined the human person as an "individual substance of rational nature." The Christian tradition, which influenced definitively the Western philosophical notion of person, was preoccupied with Christology and the doctrine of the Trinity. The Boethian definition with its emphasis on autonomy and subsistence may lead to "tritheism" instead of a Trinity where relationship is anchored on divine subsistence. Medieval attempts to modify Boethius led to an emphasis on incommunicability and singularity of existence (Richard of St. Victor), being-for-itself (or subsistent being) of intellectual nature (Aquinas), self-consciousness with a relationship or openness to God (Scotus). While the African social definition of person displays the human person as subsistent relationship—in other words, the per-

son as fundamentally "being-with," "living-with," "belonging-to"—
Western philosophy lays emphasis on the absolute originality and concreteness of the human person, a "being-for-itself." Western philosophy, right from medieval times, has recognized relationship as fundamental for the realization of the person—the universal openness of the
human person to enter into relationship with being. The importance of
the individual as a subject which is nonreducible to an object and realizes itself in relationship is also basic to phenomenology and existen-
tialism. However, Western systems wish to guard against the dissolu-
tion of the person in relationship. The "I" is already constituted before
ever it chooses to be related. The autonomy and the incommunicability of the "I" are fundamental. While the divine persons may be defined as subsistent relationship by Aquinas, humans are not seen that
way. In Western systems relationship is not constitutive of the being
of humans despite the fact that it is fundamental to human existence.[10]

While the modern notion of the human person as an individual of
sheer autonomous will whose life is the development of his or her
personality may be radically different from the medieval notions, yet
this exaggerated modern notion draws from that tradition, which emphasizes the concreteness, singularity, autonomy, and incommunicability of the human person, who, to realize the self in existence, may
choose to be related. The impact of the modern individualistic notion
of the human person is there for all to see.

In a recent very popular sociological study, *Habits of the Heart*,
Robert N. Bellah and his colleagues show the ramifications of this
individualism in American life. The dignity and sacredness of the individual are seen in American culture as the inviolable right to think,
judge, make decisions for oneself, and live one's life as one sees fit.
Any infringement of this right is "not only morally wrong" but also
"sacrilegious." The two principal dimensions of this individualism,
the study shows, are utilitarian individualism and expressive individualism. The representative figure of utilitarian individualism is the freewheeling entrepreneur or manager who uses every available rational
and technical tool to make profit for himself or for his company. Expressive individualism may be represented by the therapist at work
telling his or her client that the basis for a balance in life is first and
foremost the consultation with one's desires or sentiments. This middle-
class individualism, which has its older cultural roots in liberal Protestantism and republicanism but which in its modern pattern depends on

the political philosophy of John Locke, poses serious problems for America and the world. If the individual is prior to society, and if society emerges through the voluntary contract of individuals trying to maximize their self-interest, the survival of both society and individual become problematic. Bellah and his group sum up the difficulty in the following statement: "American cultural traditions define personality, achievement, and the purpose of human life in ways that leave the individual suspended in glorious, but terrifying, isolation."[11] Their solution is not the abandonment of individualism—this would undercut the foundations of American culture—but in finding a common language which will reconcile effectively the claims of individuality and community.

African anthropology (the doctrine of the human person) parts company with this modern Western system of thought to insist that communicability is of the very essence of the person. The autonomy and rights of the individual subject are enjoyed in relationship, in communication. Indeed the "freedom" of the individual is "for" the construction of a better community. This freedom is experienced in the free rein given to individuals to use creatively the gifts or charisms wrapped up in their particular destinies. It is not principally understood in terms of "freedom from" an oppressive society. This does not mean that oppressors are not resisted and overthrown. Rather the human person, as we have shown above, is socially defined as essentially a being (or, as some would say, a "life-ing") in relationship—*motho ke motho ka betho ka bang* (a human person is human because of others).

Creative Harmonization of African and Western Valuations of Person

In the modern world, dominated by violence and Western culture, we are not free to choose either one or the other. The exaggeration of the one leads to radical individualism, and the overemphasis of the other creates the domination of the masses by an influential segment of the community (rulers, elders, priests, mass media). Both ideas have to be creatively married. Consequently, the fight for the liberation of Saro-Wiwa should go along with the struggle for the respect of Ogoni land which has been polluted by oil companies. One should seek justice for the fishermen and farmers whose land and waters have been rendered poisonous. There should be equity in the redistribution of the oil revenue so that the reconstruction and development of the poverty-stricken villages and hamlets may be realized. Finally, the struggle for the improvement of the quality of life of the majority (of Nigerians) should be pursued with vigor in order to reduce the violence of the state and the high crime wave. In other words, the interconnections which create the human person and human communities impose moral obligations on the relationship between the individual and the community, and between communities. Christians should draw from the Jewish and Christian Scriptures elements of the relational notion of the individual person and community to help rebuild the world.

The exaggerations of Western individualism since the Enlightenment were adapted within Christianity to the point where Christian faith as a matter of individual decision and application became one of the hallmarks of Western Christianity.[12] Christian ethics became highly developed on the level of individual responsibility but was very weak on community responsibility. Christian behavior and the salvation flowing therefrom became privatized. Liberal Protestant theology, as exemplified in the authoritative work of Adolf von Harnack, *The Essence of Christianity*, reduced the specificity of the Kingdom and Christianity to the individual or private level—God and the individual soul. The church is the spiritual community which links like souls of good will but which is not identifiable in any existing community here on earth; the concern of the Jesus of the Gospels is the individual soul, and there is no relationship between the Kingdom and the involvement of the Christian community in the affairs of this world.

Catholic theology separates itself from this Kingdom theory and individualism of late nineteenth- and early twentieth-century Protestantism. But in the Catholic practice the notion of person and salvation, the manner of the administration of the sacraments, and the structures of the church testify to the dominance of the individualism current since the Enlightenment.[13] The identification of church and state, which started from the peace of Constantine, matured in the fifth century (Theodosius), and terminated with the French Revolution (1789), entrenched the denial of human rights within the church and robbed the institution of its prophetic role. The horrendous effects of the free-enterprise system and the ideology of liberalism jolted a weakened church to rediscover its prophetic role in the world, beginning with *Rerum Novarum* of Leo XIII (1891).

Today North-South relations, the power of Western finance houses and multinational corporations, and the unfettered liberty of the Western individual business person or community have turned life on this planet into hell for four-fifths of humankind. The relational notion of person must be incorporated into the definition of the individual and community to entrench ethics into international political and economic relations. It is on this basis of ethics that one may talk of the "duty of humanitarian interference" in the internal affairs of nations (John Paul II and Bernard Couchner, founder of Médicins sans Frontières). A body which is not involved in partisan politics and without an ulterior economic interest needs to emerge to act as a watchdog against the unethical enslavement and exploitation of humans and the earth. A renewed Christian community can form the nucleus of such a body for the reconstruction of the earth.

CHAPTER 4

The Church as Highest Testimony of the Renewal of the Earth

The Synod of Bishops for Africa recommended a new metaphor for the interpretation of the mystery and ministry of the Christian church on earth. The new metaphor is the "Church-as-Family." The choice of this image, as the "Message" of the Synod indicates, is linked to the church's intent to transform the unjust and violent conditions of life in our world through a new type of witness. Envy, jealousy, racism, war, division of the human race into first, second, third, and fourth worlds, cult of wealth, disparity between nations, and exploitation and humiliation of the African continent through the debt burden and unfair trade arrangements or by the media are all going to be changed when we live the church as family in the image of the trinitarian family. "We are the family of God: this is the Good News! The same blood flows in our veins, and it is the blood of Jesus Christ."[1]

This metaphor, though new, is as old as the emergence of the Christian church in the form of communities which bore witness to the resurrection of Jesus. This witness is most clearly depicted in the Christian assembly, where Jesus is proclaimed as alive. The constitution or convocation of this assembly flows from the initiative of the resurrected one. The resurrected one is the founder, the foundation and initiator, of this eschatological group. Indeed the new group is described by John's Gospel as flowing out of the very body of Jesus, who gave himself up in sacrifice unto death. The "water and blood" which flowed from his pierced side (Jn 19:34) testify to the fact that he was really dead—a death which is a voluntary sacrifice: "he handed over the spirit" (Jn 19:30). Thus his resurrection and bestowal of the

Spirit (Jn 20:22) gave birth to the new group. The Fathers of the church interpret, symbolically, the "water and blood" which came out of his "opened" side (Augustine) as the emergence of the church and her fundamental sacraments (baptism and Eucharist). The church herself (the new Eve) flows out of the side of Christ (the new Adam).[2] Through the "Spirit" which he "gave up" (Jn 19:30) and "breathed on them" (Jn 20:22), members are born by the water bath (Jn 3) and are nourished by the "bread of life" (his body and blood—Jn 6). In the fellowship or family meal where, as the head or master of the family, he pronounces the blessings over the meal, he is recognized at the "breaking of the bread," a recognition through which the church is born (Lk 24; 1 Cor 11).

This church is a real family which has God as the only Father. To underline the indispensable contribution of this new family of God in the transformation of the world of today, I shall highlight two elements: (a) only a local church which is aware of its autonomy and universal mission, based on the experience of the resurrected one, may hope to be a challenge to the world—in other words, the one church is realized and bears witness to the Christ only as local church; and (b) the ministry of service in the following of Jesus is the greatest challenge to violence and domination in the world of today.

The Autonomy of Each Local Church in the Oneness of the Catholic Church

Wherever Jesus of Nazareth, who preached the good news of the Kingdom and died for it, is recognized as alive or risen, there the church is born. Such an emergence of the church is always a communal experience. Such an experience is never outside the community and is never had by proxy. One may use the familiar example of the apparition to the disciples on their way to Emmaus (Lk 24). The stranger (the Christ) who joined them opened to them the Scriptures and showed them a new way of interpreting their life. Their hearts started burning within them. Finally, taking the initiative, they invited him to their house because it was getting late. At table, he took the place of the father of the family; and then he performed the gestures for which he is known— took bread, gave thanks, broke and gave to them. They recognized him "at the breaking of the bread"—as all communities will recognize him in that familiar foundational action. It is the arising of the church.

Their witness, which is to be linked to the testimony of the Eleven (apostles) was not inferior to but was confirmed by the Apostolic witness.[3] A similar process followed Peter's homily at Pentecost (Acts 2). Those who were moved to conversion and received baptism were bestowed with the Holy Spirit (the effects of the victory of the resurrected Jesus). They formed the church.

As soon as this faith in the resurrection is experienced, the new birth as church takes place. The new birth arises from a new relationship to the Christ in his Spirit and creates new relationships. The apostles or messengers who proclaim the good news are the instruments of the emergence of the new community. In being the authorized means of bringing a people in contact with Jesus, they are founders or builders of the church or community. For example, in the Johannine story of the conversion of the Samaritans (Jn 4), many believed in Jesus at the testimony of the woman. However, the full manifestation of the church is in the deep encounter of the Word welcomed and rooted in a particular community. This is the work of the Spirit of Jesus, the Spirit of God, a Spirit which ensures the oneness of the church and endows each particular church with a resilience to bear witness to the Kingdom, breaking down thereby the artificial barriers erected by groups and peoples. The Samaritan community took the initiative of giving hospitality to Jesus (a Jew—a stranger who is also a bringer of good luck). And through this intimate reception of the Word the local community became empowered to live and proclaim the one faith in its own right and independently of the apostle or messenger. It asserted its autonomy while manifesting its character as the one church. As the Samaritans told the messenger who proclaimed the news to them (the woman who encountered Jesus at Jacob's well), "It is no longer because of what you said that we believe, for we have heard for ourselves, and we know that this is truly the Savior of the world" (Jn 4:42).[4]

The Primacy of the Spirit

Luke shows how much the church is the product of the Spirit of God and its sphere of operation. The reconstituted Israel of God (the Twelve, completed by Matthias, Acts 1:15-16, and the disciples on whom the Spirit of Jesus was bestowed) was led by Peter on the day of Pentecost. Peter's preaching created the condition for the conversion of the repentant, who were baptized through the invocation of the name of Jesus, had their sins forgiven, and received the gift of the Holy Spirit (Acts 2:38). While the action of the church is in preaching and baptizing in the name of Jesus, the Spirit of God operative always within the church is responsible for the conversion, the forgiveness of sins, and the bestowal of the gift of the Spirit in the community.[5] The assembly thus constituted has all the necessary means of living and bearing witness to the unique experience of the risen Jesus. In this way it enjoys its autonomy. But it is always an autonomy in relationship.

Luke makes very prominent the role of the Spirit in revolutionizing the principle of relationship in his story of the conversion of the non-Jewish races. His intention seems to be to project an idealized image of the one church where all racial barriers break down. The visions of Cornelius and Peter (Acts 10-11) and the compliance of both to the order (promptings) of the Spirit succeeded in moving the Jewish-Christian community beyond the frontiers of race without minimizing the fact that the Savior of the world comes from the Jews. While Peter is the focal point of the conversion of the attitude of the Jewish Christians, Cornelius assembles the non-Jewish races. The "passivity" of both communities in their response to, or compliance with, the action of the Spirit creates the theological effect: the new covenant in the blood of Jesus for the forgiveness of sins is made available to the nations under the sovereign directive of the Spirit of God. Peter was directed to give hospitality to and receive hospitality from the nations because nothing that God has rendered clean should be called unclean.

And Peter had hardly stopped speaking when the ecstatic experience of the Spirit was bestowed on the non-Jewish races independently of the church of the circumcision. Whatever may have been the difficulties about determining the status of the law of purity for non-Jewish Christians, Lucan theology makes it clear that the Jewish church could do nothing but rejoice in amazement that the gentiles had also received the faith. It is the one faith and the one church. The Jewish church (the Jerusalem church) does not enjoy a superior faith and is thus not a superior church. Certainly it guards elements of the Jewish ritual practices but as a local custom (Acts 15). The *anteriority* in the foundation of the church of Jerusalem does not mean a *superiority* in the experience of faith in the resurrected Savior of the world.[6]

This sovereign liberty of the Spirit to open the message of the king-

dom to other races, worlds, and cultures may not be construed to have
ended with the entrance of a particular sector of the gentiles into the
one church. This appears to have been the unfortunate reading of the
facts by the Graeco-Roman church. From the time the church came
under the influence of the Graeco-Roman world, she married her theology so well with the laws, politics, and philosophy of this world that
she virtually excluded other possible versions of this same world. Thus
we have the unusual situation whereby the life of the church is made
to be responsive to the worldview of a small section of the nations and
has become intolerant of other alternatives. The local expression of
the one faith in the one church became fixed and resistant to the ecstatic action of the Spirit among other races. It was not until Vatican II
that this monocultural image of the church was understood to be harmful to the life and mission of the church. Under the direction of the
Spirit the openness to variety in the realization of the one church con-
fessing the same one faith was restored in principle. For the church in
Africa to effectively bear witness to the resurrected one in her world,
she has to guard the one experience of faith and maintain her local
autonomy in the one church.

Unity and Autonomy: The Ecclesiology of Cyprian
of Carthage

Cyprian of Carthage, in the third century of our era, and the North
African church painted a touching image of both the oneness of this
church and the autonomy of the local church in order to coherently
bear witness in a troubled world. First and foremost, the bishop of
Carthage underlined that the church is one because it arises from the
one and only source, the one and only origin. The episcopacy, or rather
the priesthood, which is one and fully enjoyed by each bishop, is, in
its unity of communion, the sign of the unity of the one church. In his
classic *The Unity of the Catholic Church* Cyprian used the imagery of
the sun's rays, the branches of a tree, and streams arising from one
source to describe the church's unity.

> The authority of the bishops forms a unity, of which each holds
> his part in its totality. And the Church forms a unity, however far
> she spreads and multiplies by the progeny of her fecundity; just
> as the sun's rays are many, yet the light is one, and a tree's

branches are many, yet the strength deriving from its sturdy root is one. So too, when many streams flow from a single spring, though their multiplicity seems scattered abroad by the copiousness of the welling waters, yet their oneness abides by reason of their starting-point. Cut off one of the sun's rays—the unity of its light permits of no division; break off a branch from the tree, it can bud no more; dam off a stream from its source, it dries up below the cut. So too the Church glowing with the Lord's light extends her rays over the whole world; but it is one and the same light which is spread everywhere, and the unity of her body suffers no division. She spreads her branches in generous growth over all the earth, she extends her abundant streams ever further; yet one is the head-spring, one the source, one the mother who is prolific in her offspring, generation after generation: of her womb are we born, of her milk are we fed, from her Spirit our souls draw their life-breath.[7]

Cyprian's theology of the unity of the many branches which make up the one church is continuous with the earliest New Testament experience of the one church. This earliest experience of *assembling in the name of Jesus* was in the form of "house-churches." Pauline letters and Acts make frequent references to such churches, which assembled in the houses of Prisca and Aquila (1 Cor 16:19; cf. Acts 18:18-19), Mary the mother of John Mark (Acts 12:12), Chloe (1 Cor 1:11), and Philemon. A common faith in the risen Lord whose Spirit guides the assembled community, a common hope, fundamental ethical principles dominated by love (agape), and the cult (especially of the Eucharist, which breaks all boundaries) bind these churches together as the one church.

There were differences in the way of being a community of believers or the new Israel of God after the resurrection of Jesus. For the Jewish-Christian group around James, the tendency was to insist on the fulfillment of the law; and there were internal divisions about how far one should go in tolerating non-Jews and in the integral fulfillment of the law. It was not evident what aspects should be considered binding for all or what should be local. In the crucial question about table fellowship and the Eucharist there was no unanimity about where the boundary between Jewish and gentile Christians should be drawn. In clear ways the churches maintained their localness (and autonomy) in the realization of their oneness. Consequently, as Brown suggests, there may have been a house-church of Christian Jews attached to the Mosaic law, a house-church of mixed Jewish and gentile Christians which did not impose circumcision on gentiles but did not relativize the value of the law in Christian life, a house-church from the Pauline mission consisting mostly of gentiles completely liberated from the law, and a Johannine house-church characterized by the insistence on being children of God and disciples of Jesus, who is present through the Paraclete.[8]

The picture which emerges from the New Testament and which is confirmed in the church of the Fathers is that the one church is recognized in its many features. The emphasis on unity may not be confused with uniformity. Indeed what is manifestly incontrovertible is the localness and autonomy of the churches. As Cyrille Vogel asserts, "Historically, the problem is not to analyze how local churches became autonomous, but rather to find out why they felt the need to regroup under larger units."[9] The division of the Eastern and Western church into various liturgical rites and families is the most eloquent testimony of the localization and autonomy of the churches in the one church. Very influential metropolitan centers, such as Rome, Alexandria, Antioch, and Constantinople, became focal points for the regrouping into larger units. In the Western church the North African church under Cyprian and after him offers a telling example of autonomy in the one church.

Cyprian's Understanding of *Concordia* among Local Churches

The importance of North Africa in giving theological leadership to the Western church is well known. Tertullian, Cyprian, and Augustine were pillars of the local North African church and the church of the West. No one pondered on the unity of the church as Cyprian; but none held to the privilege and autonomy of each church, embodied in each local bishop, as Cyprian. The Petrine privilege is the symbol of the one priesthood; and the moral unity, or communion (Cyprian uses *concordia*), among the bishops is a testimony of the unity of the one church. However, all the bishops are equal, and each is answerable to God for his ministry. "The authority of the bishops forms a unity, of which each holds his part in its totality."

During the baptismal controversy the North African church in three councils refused to recognize Novatian baptisms. All those baptized in Novatian assemblies were rebaptized in North Africa. The Roman church under Stephen I held the contrary view and imposed hands on Novatian Christians to reconcile them to the great church. Stephen's reply to Cyprian's communication about the way North Africa saw the controversy appeared truculent and authoritarian. Cyprian's communication arose from a concern for the moral unity which must always be at the service of the oneness of the church. North African ecclesiology would not recognize any juridical right of the Roman bishop over the metropolitan of Carthage or over any other bishops of North Africa. The crisis posed the danger of a real schism between Rome and North Africa. North Africa was, however, shocked that Rome threatened to break communion over such an issue. During the Seventh Council of Carthage (the third council held to deliberate the issue, with Cyprian presiding, September 1, 256) Cyprian prefaced the meeting by reminding his brother bishops of the sovereign independence of each bishop in his church. And he also insisted that in the matter under discussion liberty should be respected. One should refrain from passing judgment on those who think in a different manner; and the differences should not lead to the breaking of communion.

> It but remains that each of us should, in regard to this same matter, bring forward his opinion, judging no one, nor depriving anyone of the right of communion if he should think differently. For neither does anyone of us set himself up as a bishop, nor by tyranny and terror does anyone compel his colleagues to the necessity of obedience, since every bishop has his own free will to the unrestrained exercise of his liberty and power, so that neither can he be judged by another, nor is he himself able to judge another. Rather, let us all await the judgment of our Lord Jesus Christ, the one and only one who has both the power of setting us over the governing of His Church, and of judging our conduct in that capacity.[10]

Cyprian's position is consistent with an ecclesiology developed before the controversy: there is one church originating from one source, and there is one priesthood derived from one source. The oneness of the priesthood is demonstrated in the privilege of Peter. Despite the fact that Peter was in no way superior to the other apostles, yet the Lord made him bishop before the others to show the oneness of the priesthood which the bishops guard in solidarity. But just as each local church is a branch of the one church (autonomy and unity), each bishop is sovereign over his church but in communion with the primal see of Peter, which is the manifestation or sacrament of this unity. Once again the anteriority of Peter's bishopric in no way signifies any superiority; nor does it confer on the chair of Peter any juridical powers over the other bishops.[11]

For Cyprian, the *concordia,* or moral unity (communion), of the bishops is vital for the manifestation of the one church. Pastors must always bear in mind that there is one flock which they have been chosen to feed. Divergences in the understanding of elements of the faith or in the practice of moral discipline should not lead a pastor to break communion with another church. For example, Cyprian reproached the rigorist Novatian, who differed from Cornelius, the duly elected bishop of Rome, on the issue of the measures to be adopted for reconciling apostates in the Roman church. This was the principal reason Novatian led his party to secession and became their bishop. Cyprian pointed out in Letter 55 that in North Africa bishops from various provinces differed on the issue of whether or not to reconcile adulterers. And yet between those who held a rigorist view and those who were more lenient there was no break in communion. In the relationship of concord, or communion, the indivisible unity of the church is preserved. It is for each bishop to act as he saw fit, and to render account to God.[12]

In highlighting the quarrel over baptism, our interest is not in whether the rigorist North African position is right or wrong. Augustine was to profoundly modify this North African position. But the crucial emphasis is on the notion of the church, which is one but multiple. Each local church, as this one church, springs from the Lord and is bestowed with all the necessary means of bearing witness to the risen Lord in its context. It will always strive to maintain communion with other churches in order to manifest the oneness of this church. The practice since the earliest times of having neighboring bishops be present at the ordination of a bishop of a local church protects this communion. According to the Council of Arles there should be seven or at least three bishops but never only one bishop for the ordination of any other bishop.[13] The theology of Cyprian and the discipline of the North African church are suffused with this principle of oneness and multiplicity manifest in communion. The bishops of North Africa were firmly convinced of the truth of their position in rebaptizing Novatians. But they would not break communion with the Roman bishop over the issue. The citing of tradition by the Roman bishop was irrelevant. Tradition must be based on inner truth. According to Cyprian, Peter, who was the first of the apostles, made no claims of being the elder when Paul differed from him on the issue of circumcision. Rather he accepted the position of Paul, a new convert and a former persecutor of the church, because it was the truth. Thus the unity of the church was preserved.[14]

North African Legal Procedures and the Appeal to Rome

This principle of autonomy and communion in order to guard the unity of the one church was always kept alive in the North African church. The influential metropolitan see of Carthage was a focal point for regrouping the dioceses in Roman North Africa. In their various councils they took decisions for the well-being of their local church. The primacy of the Roman church was never questioned because it is the symbol of unity. But North Africa would not tolerate the interference of Rome in the affairs of its own church.

The North African judicial processes are the only ones to be followed. Canon 10 of the Second Council of Carthage under Genetlius (390) followed earlier conciliar decisions stating that if it was not possible to await a general assembly of the bishops, a tribunal of twelve bishops would suffice for the trial of a bishop. And the Council of Hippo (October 8, 393) clarified the procedure: the court of first instance is under the primate of a province, while the court of appeal is the general assembly of the churches of Africa, which meets annually. There is no appeal against the decisions of the general assembly.

Justice is rendered to priests, deacons, and the minor clergy. Priests and deacons are tried by six and three bishops respectively (the bishop of the accused being one of the judges—Second Council of Carthage). The minor clergy are judged by their bishops alone. Furthermore, the council of May 1, 418, in which 200 bishops participated, stated that priests, deacons, and minor clergy have a right of appeal to the primate of the province or to the general council of the provinces of Africa. In this way, the justice accorded to bishops was also extended to the other members of the clergy. And the council went ahead to excommunicate anyone who would appeal to Rome, since North Africa had within its territory all that was necessary for the administration of justice.

Indeed, when certain bishops and other clergy formed the habit of crossing the Mediterranean to take their problems to the emperor or to the Roman pope, the Twentieth Council of Carthage (fifth century) reacted. A canon of this council (attested in 525) separated from communion anyone who would bypass the normal canonical regulations in vigor on various levels of the church in the region to appeal to the Roman church—"ut nullus ad Romanam ecclesiam audeat appellare" (let no one dare to appeal to the Roman church).[15]

Roman Patriarchal Power as Distinct from Papal Primacy

The privilege of Peter is not to be confused with the papal juridical metropolitan and patriarchal power. The Spanish, Franco-Germanic, English, and Irish churches had autonomous control of their life as local church in the eighth century while at the same time supporting the primacy of Rome. But with the close identification of church and state which started at the time of Constantine, and especially with the use of civil power to impose decisions of councils, the liberty of the local church in the West was gradually reduced. When Charlemagne became emperor in the ninth century, the unification of liturgies and the unification of the empire were indistinguishable. Consequently, the very influential Gallican liturgies (in use in Franco-Germanic countries) in principle ceased to exist in order to put in place what Congar called the Carolingian ideology of unity: one God, one empire, one emperor, one pope, one law, one ritual. This confusion between unity and uniformity was sealed in the eleventh century during the reform of Gregory VII. The Spanish liturgy ceased to exist. The West became simply Latin; the local bishop was gradually reduced to a representative of the Roman pope. Gradually also all the local churches became incorporated into the local church of Rome, so that the idea of multiplicity in the one church was totally lost. "The urban community of Rome integrated into the small space of its *urbs* (city) the whole Latin world (*orbis*)" (von Allmen). In brief, the West became one local community and lost the aspect of unity in plurality.[16]

It is this uniform local community of the West which was brought into sub-Saharan Africa during the colonial period, as I already pointed out above. Apart from the colonial ideology shared by the missionaries, there was an added burden of a uniformist ecclesiology. It is not surprising that in Africa we live in a church which is dependent at all levels and which is turned towards Rome—a church which, from the start, was ignorant of its autonomy as a local church in the one church.

One may, then, appreciate the very courageous work of Vatican II to restate the theology of the church, from its New Testament origins to the Fathers of the church. But insofar as the uniformist ecclesiology prevalent before the council is not radically changed and is embodied in relevant canons, the capacity of the local church in Africa to bear witness in her context as the one church of Christ will be very limited. When Cardinal Hyacinthe Thiandoum of Dakar (Senegal) proclaimed, in the 1994 Synod of Bishops for Africa, that liturgies such as the Zairian rite approved by the Holy See are not "a concession" but "a right,"[17] he was underlining a crucial area in the realization of the one but multiple church in its local setting. To realize such local churches in Africa, there must be a redefinition of the relationship or communion of churches in the Western church.

The African Local Church in Relationship to the Western Church

We are not in the New Testament period, nor are we living in the time of Cyprian of Carthage. But these periods must help us to critique the anomaly of the historical centralization of the church in the West, linked to the local Western sociocultural and political developments. In this historical development of the Western church, the church assumed the shape of the state. This influence of the social organization of the Graeco-Roman state on the church is inescapable insofar as the Word must become incarnate in the human context, insofar as the church as an institution must be limited in its structure in time and space. But the goal is ultimately the transformation of this temporal order through the prophetic Word.

From the ecclesiology of Luke in the Acts of the Apostles, we learn that it is not necessary to force local practices of a sister church, derived from her interaction with her world, on converts coming from another cultural background and another local experience of the world. Thus it is not necessary for the church in Africa to carry the burden of medieval Christianity which the local church of the West finds difficult to off-load.

For a redefinition of the relationship between the local churches of Africa and the Western church to take place, it must be strongly affirmed that the Western pattern of being church is an experience of a local church. It must also be strongly affirmed that the influence of the Roman pope and the Roman church on the rest of the non-Western peoples evangelized by Western missionaries is to a great extent that of a patriarchal church. In other words, the Roman program of centralization does not arise necessarily from the ministry of unity of the office of Peter. For, as Cardinal Ratzinger has said, the image of a centralized state which the Catholic church presented up to the Second Vatican Council does not simply flow from the office of Peter but rather from this office being linked with the patriarchal duty of the bishop of Rome for Latin Christianity, which kept on increasing in the course of history.[18] In brief, the redefinition of relationship implies the adoption of a necessary distance by the church in Africa towards the Latin patriarchate, without prejudice to the primacy of the chair of Peter. This distance is necessary to maintain the tension between autonomy and communion in the one church.

Churches Fully Responsive to Local African Needs

The relationship between the Western world and Africa since the time of slavery has been characterized by exploitation. As I pointed out above, Christianity participated in this exploitation. This led to the unhappy outcome of Africa turning towards the interests and objectives of the West. This response to the external stimuli of the West functioned fully in the church. And in this enterprise both the church and the colonial government were very successful. Indigenes of Africa were placed in roles of responsibility to continue to respond to the wishes of the center. The church of Rome alone determined the choice of bishops; and the regulations guiding the organization of the church from the parish level through the diocesan to the supralocal level are determined by Rome's law. Annual returns from the bishops, *ad limina* visits, and the overbearing presence of the pro-nuncios are several ways in which pastors of African local churches respond and give account to the center. In political terms, the Catholic church in Africa is clearly under colonial administration. This anomaly prevents the pastors of the local churches from calmly seeing, judging, and making decisions about issues relevant to the life and witness of the local church.

For the Catholic church in Africa to fully respond to the needs of the context, the authority of the bishop must be clearly asserted as the focal point of the unity of the local church. The assertion of Cyprian against his opponents is here apposite: "You must understand that the bishop is in the church and the church in the bishop."[19] This responsibility is a sign of the maturity of the local church which says to the sister churches that brought her the message of the gospel, "It is no longer because of what you said that we believe, for we have heard for ourselves, and we know that this is truly the Savior of the world" (Jn 4:42).

Today, this full responsibility of the local churches in Africa in bearing witness to the Word must be assumed with all its consequences. It is fully in harmony with the description by Vatican II of the context where "the church reveals herself most clearly"—in other words, where there is the full and active participation of the holy People of God in the same liturgical celebrations, especially in the same Eucharist, in the same prayer, around the same altar where the bishop presides, surrounded by his presbyterium and ministers.[20] This description of the church is inspired by the Old Testament and New Testament experience of the church (*qahal-ekklesia*) as an assembly effectively convoked to hear the Word of God (e.g., Deut 4:10; 9:10; 10:4) or to keep the memory of Jesus, as in the house-churches frequently referred to by Paul and Luke. The full recognition given to patriarchates by Vatican II indicates the natural way in which the church in Africa should assume her legitimate autonomy in communion.

Churches Assuming the Necessary Power to Define Their Needs

The redefinition of the church in Africa in her relationship to the Western church based on autonomy and communion is today ineluctable. There appears to be no other way of fully receiving Vatican II in its letter and spirit. Those who fear that such an autonomy of the Catholic church in Africa might end up in schisms are here invited to reexamine their fears. The real fear is that of the loss of power.

The relationship between the churches of Africa and the Roman technocracy raises the issue of power. The whole debate on inculturation, which has been the dominant theme of theology in Africa and which the 1994 Synod of Bishops for Africa supports as the organizational metaphor for evangelization, is finally an issue of power. Who decides how the church should live in the context of Africa? Who makes decisions about marriage, liturgy, canon law, spirituality, and theology? The Roman technocracy which interferes in the free experience of the life of the church in particular contexts of Africa is not qualified to do so. The pro-nuncio whose opinion carries more weight in the Roman scheme of things than the pastor of a diocese is not really qualified to speak for the church. The assembly effectively convoked to listen to the Word of God and to keep the memory of Jesus, the community which welcomes the Word and proclaims and bears testimony to him as the Savior of the world must not be confused with the offices of congregations or secretariats in Rome nor with a pro-nuncio who does not preside over an assembly.

Let my remarks not be misunderstood. I am not saying that the Roman legate or pro-nuncio has no place in the present context of the church in the world and the exercise of the office of the Roman primacy. I am not saying that the Roman congregations and secretariats, which compare well with any Western technocracy (more efficient than the European Union or the United Nations, not to mention the Organization of African Unity), have no role in the communion of churches. What I am saying is that these offices are secondary (subordinate) to the realization of the one church. First and foremost, the church as assembly has to live her life in a given context. It does so by giving full hospitality to the Word (to the Stranger who makes our hearts burn within us) in order to mobilize the community for its mission. In the process of searching for the moral unity which manifests the one church, the Roman curia, which testifies to a locally tested experience, may make its invaluable contribution. But it cannot replace the responsibility of the pastors of churches nor make decisions for their contextual witness to the Kingdom. The curia cannot render an account to God of the ministry of the pastors.

My position may raise difficulties in the redefinition of the relationship of the local churches in Africa to the sister Roman church. But this is not new. Both the Roman church and the bishops of Africa are fully aware of these difficulties. While the bishops of Africa (regrouped under the Symposium of Episcopal Conferences of Africa and Madagascar [SECAM] or under national conferences) are in favor of greater autonomy and responsibility, the Roman church with its bureaucracy is interested in imposing a speed limit. The issue of inculturation demonstrates these parallel interests.

Inculturation or Power at the Center

The period after Vatican Council II saw a lot of creativity in the Catholic church in Africa. One may refer to the Ndzon-Melen Mass of Yaoundé, the Zairian rite, the eucharistic liturgies in East Africa, and the Mossi initiation rite in Burkina Faso. The Roman pontiffs Paul VI and John Paul II showed delight in these experiments and admitted legitimate plurality in the realization of the church. Paul VI was, however, careful to limit this plurality to the manner of expressing the faith (language, style, and so on). This is the limit of his African Christianity (Kampala, Uganda, 1969)! The Christian message as the church had formulated and fixed it in definite concepts and words is untouchable!

The bishops who listened to the pontiff that same year, when SECAM was created, happily went home to create "an African Christianity" and to be "missionaries to themselves." Five years later, during the Fourth Synod of Bishops on Evangelization (1974), they made a declaration calling for evangelization in coresponsibility. They gave their full support to a specifically African theology. They even set aside the prevalent theology of adaptation in favor of a theology of incarnation. The Word must become flesh in Africa! In other words, there must be in Africa a contextual interpretation of the experience of Jesus, with the risks of errors and heresies. As Archbishop Zoa put it humorously: "Allow us to err. You yourselves have had 2000 years to err."

The pastoral experience of our bishops persuaded them to decide that whatever be the position of the Roman pope, the pluralism of contexts and theologies affirmed since Vatican II must be upheld. A contextual theology on the continent of Africa was not negotiable.

Paul VI, in his closing discourse of the synod of 1974, warned against the danger of talking about theologies according to continents and cultures. And in 1975, in another address to SECAM, he clearly underlined that there was no question of exercising "freedom" or "autonomy" in theological research outside the *communio ecclesiae*. This position may be difficult to fault. But the burning issue is the definition or redefinition of this communion. *Communio ecclesiae* in the thinking and declarations of African bishops is not understood as being confined to the straitjacket of a uniform Roman local church-community.[21]

On his part, John Paul II has supported the move towards acculturation or inculturation in the churches of Africa. Through this process Christ will become incarnate within the very heart of African life, and the totality of African life will be brought to Christ. Consequently, Christ in the members of his Body will become African. The churches of Africa will certainly say "Amen"! But when the pope comes to the more precise issue of the Zairian liturgy and the norms necessary for its application, he limits himself to those sections of *Sacrosanctum Concilium* (Constitution on the Sacred Liturgy) of Vatican II which cover simple adaptations (nos. 37-38). It is worthy of note that the paragraph of the constitution which foresees more profound adaptations or a move away from the "unity of the Roman rite" (no. 40) was never cited by the pope in any of his speeches in Africa. This omission has to be interpreted as deliberate. The context of Africa and the requests of the local churches for more autonomy in liturgical matters should naturally have led the pope to support such requests by citing that relevant paragraph. As the council Fathers declared:

> In some places and circumstances, however, an even more radical adaptation of the liturgy is needed and entails greater difficulties.
>
> Therefore:
>
> (1) The competent territorial ecclesiastical authority mentioned in Article 22, par. 2, must, in this matter, carefully and prudently consider which elements from the traditions and genius of individual peoples might appropriately be admitted into divine worship. Adaptations which are judged to be useful or necessary should then be submitted to the Apostolic See, by whose consent they may be introduced. (no. 40)

I am inclined to think that the omission of this radical dimension of adaptation by the pope is not accidental.

Recently, the Sacred Congregation for Divine Worship and the Discipline of the Sacraments published a document, "The Roman Liturgy and Inculturation."[22] This was barely a week and a half before the African synod. Despite the fact that the text was ready and approved for publication on January 25, 1994, the timing of its publication on March 30, 1994, could hardly be interpreted as unconnected with the Special Assembly of the Synod of Bishops for Africa which opened on April 10, 1994. Inculturation is *the* burning issue in the African church. The document describes inculturation in the limited Roman perspective of adaptation. It says that "the work of inculturation does not foresee the creation of new families of rites" (no. 36). But we know from liturgical history that there is a proliferation of rites within given liturgical families.[23] Consequently, within the family of the Roman type, differentiated African rites (like a Romano-Zairian rite) are legitimate.

However, the intent of the recent document on inculturation is to impose limits on creativity. Its restricted interpretation of *Sacrosanctum Concilium*, no. 40, on "an even more radical adaptation" states clearly that "adaptations of this kind do not envisage a transformation of the Roman rite, but are made within the context of the Roman rite" (no. 63). In other words, the congregation is interpreting "more radical adaptations" (*Sacrosanctum Concilium*, no. 40) as subordinated to maintaining the "substantial unity of the Roman rite" (*Sacrosanctum Concilium*, no. 38). If this is the only valid interpretation of this crucial number of the document of Vatican II on the liturgy, one is at a loss to understand why the Fathers of the council found it necessary to address the issue of "radical adaptations" at all. If one does not want to fall back into the strict uniformity and rigidity that characterized the Tridentine missal of Pius V (a uniformity which the same document, "The Roman Liturgy and Inculturation," regrets—no. 17), one must appreciate the legitimate interpretation of *Sacrosanctum Concilium*, no. 40, to include the emergence of differentiated rites within the loose federation of a Roman (Western) liturgical family. When one admits fully that Greek and Latin cultural areas are more closely related to each other than the African sociocultural area to any one of them, one may not need too much imagination to foresee the emergence of rites which are legitimate Christian transformations of the received Roman rite. It appears to me that Cardinal Thiandoum's remark about Africa's right to have its rites must be read in the sense of these transformations. And it is my guess that the publication of the document on inculturation by the Congregation for Divine Worship and the Discipline of the Sacraments may have been done to preempt any radical recommendations during the African synod.

I am persuaded by the above examples to assert that both the Roman church authorities and the leadership of the churches of Africa are well aware of the implications of the move towards autonomy. SECAM has made insistent demands for more responsibility and autonomy. The Roman church leadership does not appear disposed to grant such autonomy.[24] The historic assertion of Cardinal Thiandoum in his general report to the 1994 Synod for Africa that particular rites for African local churches are a "right" instead of a "concession" shows that autonomy is still a burning issue. Whatever may be the feelings of the Roman bureaucracy, the Catholic church in Africa is set on an irreversible route of redefining the terms of relationship or communion with the Roman church.

CHAPTER 5

The "Church Family": Facilitator
of Relationship in an Interdependent World

The redefinition of relationship in the Christian "commonwealth" (Tertullian) will benefit from the new program or metaphor of the church as "family of God" proposed by the Synod of Bishops for Africa. This new metaphor adopted by African bishops wishes to introduce into the life of the church the caring and warmth characteristic of the multiple channels or links of kin relationship grouped under the term "family" in Africa. In our "church-family" we are brothers and sisters because we have the same Mother and the same Father. The matter was theorized and lived from the New Testament down to the Fathers of the church. We have one God for our Father, and one church for our Mother. As Cyprian beautifully put it in his Letter 74—despite its polemical context: "As the birth of Christians takes place in baptism, the generation and sanctification do not happen outside the Spouse of Christ, who alone could give birth spiritually and give children to God. . . . To be able to have God as Father, one must first of all have the Church for mother."[1]

The idea of church as family should, however, not be construed to mean that the African cultural experience will set the terms for the construction of this "new family of God." On the contrary! One already notices this tendency in the synod's "Message to the People of God" when it links the notion of family with the spiritual "paternity" of its priests. This metaphor must be stripped of all the characteristics of patriarchal dominance. The novelty of the gospel must predominate.

The novelty of the gospel introduces a mode of being into the African family experience similar to the way Jesus lived family life in order to reassemble the new family of God or new People of God based on a new kind of relationship. This may not exclude division (Lk 12:52f); and it will certainly include an openness that knows no limits (Mk 3:31-35).

Negatively, the church-family in which we live is not an association of clans and ethnic groups, but a brotherhood and sisterhood beyond the frontiers of blood relationship, clan, ethnic group, or race. A primordial uprooting is needed in order to be admitted to membership in this new family.

> Jesus said, "Truly I tell you, there is no one who has left house or brothers or sisters or mother or father or children or fields, for my sake and for the sake of the good news, who will not receive a hundredfold now in this age—houses, brothers and sisters, mothers and children, and fields, with persecutions—and in the age to come eternal life" (Mk 10: 29-30).

It was neither chance nor forgetfulness on the part of the evangelists that led to the exclusion of "fathers" from the new family of God. Rather, according to Lohfink, here we have a clear signal of "the end of the fathers": "They are too much of a symbol of patriarchal domination." It is for this reason that Matthew insists in a polemical context, "And call no one your father on earth, for you have one Father—the one in heaven" (Mt 23:9).[2]

Tertullian rightly pointed out that people are not born Christian, that rather they are made Christian. Yet the imagery of birth (of water and the Holy Spirit [Jn 3]) is the most happy metaphor of Christian initiation because of the dynamics of the passage into being a Christian, and the warmth and caring which characterize this new family of God. But the conversion required in baptism, according to the 1994 African synod, "overcomes all particularisms and excessive ethnocentrism."[3] One should add that the conversion overcomes all manner of domination, especially patriarchal domination.

Positively, all those born into this church-family through water and the Spirit, coming from whatever race or nation, are bonded together through the victory or blood of the Lamb. They all join together to sing,

You are worthy to take the scroll
and to open its seals,
for you were slaughtered and by your blood
    you ransomed for God
saints from every tribe and language and people
    and nation;
you have made them to be a kingdom and priests
    serving our God,
and they will reign on earth (Rev 5:9-10).

The new birth into the church-family creates new relationships of warmth, acceptance, dialogue, and trust.[4] Described in the biblical as well as the African relational notion of person, the neonates (newly baptized) are linked to the church in which they are baptized, and linked to the Holy Spirit, who dwells in them to make them children of God (Rom 5:5; 8:9, 14-16). Through these channels of relationship they become participants in the Christ, members of God's household (Heb 3:6, 14) or of the Body of Christ (1 Cor 12:12-13, 27; Rom 12:4-5). They each enjoy an intimacy with the Holy Spirit, who prays in each Christian (Rom 8:15-16) and who bestows diverse gifts or charisms for the upbuilding of the community (1 Cor 12; Rom 12:4-8).

Far from degenerating into sects or a theater for the operation of primitive sentiments of nepotism, ethnocentrism or racism, the church-family, with the Holy Spirit as the motor, is a caring community guided by the Spirit to witness to the coming of the Reign of God by over-coming precisely these narrow divisions. The metaphor of the church-family is connected to the church as the new Israel of God. Indeed it may be called the fulfillment of the prophecy of the assembling of the nations on the mountain of the house of God devoid of divisions, humiliations, and violence, because this new family of Jacob, directed by the Spirit of God, walks in the light of God (Isa 2:1-4; Mic 4:1-3; cf. Acts 10-11; 15). According to Lohfink, this church-family forms an alternative society which transforms the world by its life.[5]

In this chapter, I shall show how the caring and warmth which characterize relationship in the family of God challenge the model of secular institutions precisely through the ongoing renewal of relationship among the churches and through the witness of the church as an agent of change. Instead of keeping the churches and Africa turned toward the West for all their needs, the caring for one another and the upbuilding of one another (1 Thess 5:11; 1 Cor 12:25; Gal 5:13; 6:2; etc.)[6] underscore the respect of the "somebodyness" of one another (through self-reliance) and promote the virtues of solidarity, mutuality, and interdependence. From New Testament times this mutuality and solidarity assumed a concrete image in the aid sent to the churches in need. Paul considered it a priority to collect money for the needy church of Jerusalem (1 Cor 16:1; 2 Cor 8-9). And the Roman church in the early centuries was known for her care for the less fortunate churches. Lohfink is of the view that what was uppermost in the mind of Ignatius of Antioch when he addressed the Roman church as holding "the presidency of love" was precisely the question of *agape*: the community of Rome set the pace in what constituted the essence of the church—fraternal love.[7]

The Reappraisal of Aid in the Church-Family: Self-Reliance and Interdependence

The present-day experience of donor-receiver nations, or donor-receiver churches, raises difficulties about the responsibility and autonomy of the nations and local churches of Africa. The planned extroversion of the economies of Africa since the colonial and the postcolonial periods has entrenched poverty and dependency as ways of life for the countries of Africa. This has made begging the most lucrative occupation on the continent. The continent carries the despicable image of being the only one which cannot solve its problems. Hidden by the smoke screen of want and poverty, corrupt and incompetent African governments collude with Western financial institutions to mortgage the future of generations of yet unborn Africans. The debt scandal, which the recently concluded Synod of Bishops for Africa decried, is the most telling illustration of how parents eat sour grapes and the children's teeth are set on edge. It is the crime of adults eating the food reserved for children. The situation defies solution. A certain fatalism or pessimism seems to hang over the continent. One appears to be resigned to the fact that Africa is a continent of beggars. Churches and other nongovernmental organizations have become full-time beggars. The churches of Germany appear to set the tone today of *agape,* or fraternal love. Some of the church organizations appear to be careful to respect the dignity of the needy—or, rather, beggar—churches.

However, since nothing is as alienating as begging, the relationship between the churches of Africa and the sister churches of the West has to be redefined on the basis of self-reliance, mutuality, solidarity, and interdependence. First and foremost, the economic problems which beset the continent in such apocalyptic proportions came by way of the political and cultural disorganization of the continent, as shown above. The phenomenal victory of Europe over Africa installed the unhappy principle that might is right; it entrenched violence and deceit as the vices of success. As we have often repeated, Christians were fully involved in this unhappy adventure. John Paul II has apologized for Christian Europe. Some German theologians and church leaders added their voices to regret the role of the West in the pauperization of Africa. The cooperation between our churches, as is required in the "new family of God," will begin with a lucid redefinition of the needs of Africa and the most effective ways of realizing such needs. As I have maintained in this study, the fundamental need of Africa is to reconstruct itself from its own resources.

Reviewing the Question of Loans and Aid to Africa ·

Nothing is as alienating as begging and dependency. Aid is alienating. As the recent Pan-African Congress, held in Kampala, Uganda (April 1994), and the meeting of the Organization of African Unity held a few months later in Tunisia affirmed, Africa needs to take charge of herself positively and not wait for others to solve her problems. She must be "self-centered" instead of turned towards the needs of the West.

This leads me to assert that Africa does not need the kind of aid and "soft" loans it is receiving from the West at the present time. This assertion needs to be lucidly examined. As Kamgang remarked, the phenomenon of unparalleled distress from the time Africa started receiving Western aid and loans is a sufficient argument against continuing such a practice (Kamgang, *Au-delà de la Conférence nationale,* pp. 17-47). But the reappraisal of aid must be based on the awareness of the cupidity or greed which has been entrenched as the style of rulership in Africa and the third world. Put negatively, the greedy postcolonial rulers or juntas who have held on to power or who have seized power since the 1960s are incompetent to administer the resources of Africa. Consequently, they should receive no aid on behalf of Africa. Their interest (their god) is their stomach! And their crime is double: they are not only robbers; they are destructive robbers. They rob the countries they rule, and instead of using their loot to establish industries in Africa, they buy up medieval castles in Europe, skiing resorts in Switzerland, streets in Belgium, or simply lodge the money in classified accounts in Swiss or other Western banks.

The Western banks and governments are well aware that two-thirds of the loans/aid they give return to them as stolen money—euphemistically called capital flight.[8] How can nonpatriots who are totally corrupt administer what is supposed to lift the continent out of its economic illness? How are they supposed to sign their own death warrant? Thus, I agree with Kamgang that the principal aid that the countries of the West should give us is to leave us alone and take away with them dictators they imposed on us through military might and the politics of the stomach, which have kept Africa weak since independence (Kamgang, p. 45). Western governments are fully aware of the corruption and immorality of those they are supporting in Africa. These Western governments know where their hidden accounts are lodged. These stolen monies are carefully protected by law under the smoke screen of the inalienable right of the individual to privacy. But let such African governments fall foul of the political or ideological interests of the West, such as the Libya of Maummar Khadaffi or the Iraq of Saddam Hussein, or become scapegoats for the achievement of higher ideological interests, such as Manuel Noriega of Panama, and these same Western governments quickly forget the right to individual privacy and freeze both national and individual assets. All is fair in war! The image of the freewheeling unfettered predatory capitalist, "the robber baron," investing all his technical rationality in the untrammelled pursuit of wealth without regard to the demands of social justice,[9] is in many ways the collective image the West presents to the rest of the world when its interests are at stake. Africans should no longer be deceived by the rhetoric of aid and soft loans. This kind of aid must be denounced, rejected, and fought by governments, churches, and nongovernmental organizations as inimical to the very survival of Africa.

The continent of Africa is rich not only in natural resources but also in human resources. I have already shown how the cultural and institutional traditions of Africa should be modernized to reconstruct the continent. With the establishment of a true democratic process, which consults with citizens at various levels, and with true political and cultural independence with its primary aim the political and economic unity of the continent and the removal of the artificial colonial boundaries, the continent as one nation will be set on the road to greatness. The continent should become self-centered and work for its own interests instead of responding simply to the interests of the West. This involves a reeducation of African youth: a reeducation in self-confidence, hard work, self-reliance, self-sacrifice, virtue, and uprightness; a reeducation of the masses of Africa to consume less in order to invest in the future—the future of their youth. People of character such as Martin Luther King, Jr., Kwame Nkrumah, Marcus Garvey, Gandhi, Malcolm X, Cardinal Malula, Julius Nyerere, Nelson Mandela, and Olusegun Obasanjo must be presented to the youth as models to imitate. The sacrifices of the martyrs of Uganda—young people, laypeople, Protestant and Catholic, possessed with the singleness of purpose to witness to the Kingdom—should be presented as the courageous way to create the new family of Jesus.

Freedom and faith in democratic institutions, and morality and transparency in national and international relations, especially in economic relations, are the prerequisites for the emergence of such a renewed Africa. It is in the context of such a renewed social, economic, and political culture that one may meaningfully talk of aid/loans in terms of interdependence. Programs similar to the Marshall Plan should not aim at the continued enslavement of Africa but the launching of a continent of hope free from superpower interference, free from the control of utilitarian individualism, a continent which will do business with the rest of the world on the basis of mutuality, interdependence, and the respect of the humanity and rights of communities and individuals.

The Church-Family as Agent of a New Utopia

The above program may sound utopian and unrealizable in the hurly-burly of life of the real world of economics and politics. But it is here that the relationship between our churches as the new family of God may be fully displayed for the emergence of an alternative society, for the realization of a new utopia for Africa and for the world. The church, whether on a local or on a supralocal level, does not exist for herself. She is there to bear witness to the Reign of God, to manifest the transformation of the world. The marginalization of Africa in the world today, the poverty, wars, and distress that I evoke are not chance events. They are not "accidents of history." They were planned by our conquerors to keep the continent under dependency in order to maximize the exploitation of its human and natural resources. We are faced with a situation of structural evil.

The efficiency of international capitalism and bureaucratic individualism is unquestionable. Individual Christians are powerless before it and may simply conform to it. The church, as an organization cutting across nations and peoples, may be able to achieve very little if she considers herself as a collection of individuals. But if the nature and mission of the church-family are understood in terms of relatedness, as building bridges across races and nations, as a true "ministry of reconciliation," the relationship or communion between the churches of Africa and the West assumes new dimensions in order to defend the weak and create a new world order. Convinced that the cause of defending the weak against oppressive structures is a crucial service of the Reign of God, the church-family may adopt two procedures. In the first place, she can operate with the efficient communications system of the modern world to mobilize public opinion in favor of her cause for the weak. Second, she can work from the inside to reeducate the West in particular and the world at large to correct the excesses of radical individualism in order to build a humane community where relatedness is a fundamental principle—"a human person is essentially human because of other humans."

Involving the Church in Networking

Many associations in the Western world are committed to fighting the excesses of individualism manifested in politics and economy, without going to the extent of imposing their views on others. When the relationship between our sister churches is understood in terms of the concern and warmth that predominate in the family, public opinion will be mobilized in the four corners of the globe to show coherently and persuasively the link between the political and economic interests of Western governments and the wars and distress in many parts of Africa and the world. Such networking, which is facilitated today by the phenomenal advances in information technology, cannot be overemphasized.

The first law of solidarity among our churches is communication.

Events in the oil-polluted streams and lands of the Ogoni which permit the construction of palatial villas in Ikoyi (Lagos) and Abuja (Nigeria) should be publicized; horror images of the gun-toting Rwandan government troops and militia—trained and armed by the French military—butchering and terrorizing children, women, and men should be communicated in their historical perspective to quiescent assemblies in the church of Sacré Coeur (Paris); incredible stories of the huge amounts of money from poverty-stricken and debt-riddled African nations salted away in Swiss banks should be revealed to the tranquil and rich Swiss churches. This vital information will remain unknown and, consequently, will not move the Christian assembly to responsible action unless an efficient communications network is established.

We know today that what the barons of the mass media decide should preoccupy the conscience and the consciousness of the world becomes news. Many official documents, representing the position of the Holy See, especially since Vatican II, have pointed out the evil effects of the present world economic order, which is dominated by Western capitalism. One may cite Paul VI's *Populorum Progressio* and John Paul II's *Sollicitudo Rei Socialis* as courageous voices against the exploitation of poor nations by rich ones. The U.S. Catholic Conference has also published a well-researched study adopting a position highly critical of Western capitalism, dominated by the United States. We have also noted the positions of African episcopal conferences and the recently concluded Synod of Bishops for Africa on the root causes of the distress in most African countries today. These declarations are quickly forgotten when there is no concerted plan of disseminating this information in an accessible language and when there is no program of action to change the structures that produce our misery. The time has come to pass from rhetoric to more constructive action.

The aim of the church is to advance the coming of the Reign of God which is already being realized in the assembling of the People of God. The family of God with its worldwide links of *agape*, or fellowship, must struggle for the coming of this Reign by denouncing the governments and companies which support oppressive regimes and inhuman programs for political and economic gains. This family of God not only must denounce the banks in which stolen money from Africa is lodged but must mobilize investors to boycott such banks or financial institutions. One may not underestimate the impact of such sanctions or such mobilization of Christians and other concerned people to demonstrate against companies and governments in order to realize a change in policy. The politician is interested in his or her constituency, the company manager and directors are interested in their profit. The network communications system will ensure the endangering of such limited political and economic interests through the mass mobilization of public opinion for the wider interests of humane living. But for an effective launch of such a project, the justice, peace, and human-rights groups within and outside the church must be closely linked. It means that our churches—Catholic and Protestant—must cooperate with nongovernmental organizations such as Amnesty International, Human Rights Watch, Transparency International, Médicins Sans Frontières, provided these are not used as screens for further exploitation. It also means that Christians must establish their own counterespionage to penetrate all levels of governments and companies. It is a war for the survival of humanity, a revolution in favor of humane living. It is a daunting type of witness which can only be done by a church which considers herself a family of God, a church which considers herself an alternative society. With the modern revolution in information technology, however, this mission should not be considered so daunting.

In summary, the solidarity between the churches of Africa and those of the West should first of all be felt on the level of the political and economic systems of the West, which are productive of wars and distress in faraway lands. Home governments, politicians, the business community, and the mass media must be made aware of the impact of their policies on other human beings in Africa.

Between 1977 and 1982 the church and the business community in Switzerland established an ongoing Church-Business Discussion Group. They adopted principles, or "theses," of operation in a document entitled *Churches and Business Enterprises in a World of Tension.*[10] The group is committed to the humanity of the women and men living in those countries whose cultures, politics, and economies differ from those of Switzerland—the countries in which Swiss businesses and missionaries operate. The document is a move in the right direction to entrench ethics in business. But while it foresees the withdrawal of companies in those situations where business relations morally support or directly favor a continued and severe breach of human rights, it says nothing about the impact of the Church-Business Dis-

cussion Group at home. This is an unfortunate omission, given the
notoriety of Switzerland as the haven for the shady deals of African
tyrants and dictators. Still, setting up such a discussion group already
provides structures for churches to influence the business community.
A similar objective is pursued by the Africa Faith and Justice Network, based in Washington, D.C., in the United States. Made up mainly
of Catholic religious congregations with personnel serving in Africa,
it "seeks to change structures and policies originating in the U.S. which
have adverse effect on African peoples." It identifies issues, researches
them, and presents information to its members to be considered for
advocacy.[11] A branch of this network has been established in Rome.

The intention of the missionary congregations in establishing the
Africa Faith and Justice Network is laudable. It may have started to
produce some results. But what I am proposing is at the same time
more extensive and more inclusive. The whole church as family of
God, whether assembled in Washington or Nairobi, should be sensi-
tized about the importance of such interchurch links. Dioceses, national episcopal conferences, continental conferences, the Western patriarchate, the Petrine ministry, and all the organizations that make up
the church must see in this program of networking a privileged aspect
of their witness to the Reign of God in our time in order to overcome
the oppression of the weak. The church does not exist for herself, but
for the establishment of the Kingdom. When the network is firmly
established at all these levels, and issues are discussed and consider-
ations for advocacy proposed without prejudice to local autonomy,
then one may hope to arrive at concrete realizations which are aimed
at the changing of the face of the earth. It is, in my view, the clearest
way of showing the pertinence of the church in the world of today. It
is a war to stop all wars, to stop all bloodshed, to put an end to misery
and begging.

The struggle should involve all people of good will, but especially
it should define the vocation of all Christians, whatever be their de-
nomination. Christians should no longer live in tranquillity in any part
of the world while there is suffering and pain anywhere in the world.
The church of the early centuries (before the Peace of Constantine)
found it difficult to accommodate wars and bloodshed in her rank and
file. Tertullian argued that if John the Baptist welcomed soldiers and
if the centurion was converted, Jesus put an end to the carrying of
arms and to military service when he "disarmed Peter" in the garden

of Gethsemane. But the most potent argument is proposed by Origen: Christians constitute a new family, a new people, a new generation, a new priesthood—consequently, an alternative society. In his famous reply to Celsus, Origen argued that temple priests of the Graeco-Roman world never soiled their hands with blood, and were never recruited for war. (One could compare this to the horror the Nri-Igbo of Nigeria have for bloodshed. The priestly group of the Nri sought to pacify the earth with rituals of purification.) The Christian priestly people, according to Origen, is an eminent and sacred body. While others fought wars as soldiers, they fight as priests and servants of God. They keep their hands pure and raise them in prayer to God for those who wage just wars and who rule justly. Thus the alternative Christian society constructs a new world order.[12]

In redefining the relationship between our churches of Africa and the Western churches, I emphasize the involvement of the churches in overcoming structures that create wars, poverty, and oppression. Let me repeat, it is important to denounce wars and massacres in Rwanda and Angola, but it is more important to uproot the causes of these evils. The community of believers all over the world, open to one another and under the direction of the Spirit, is a consecrated and priestly people. Its hands will not be tainted with blood. But it raises its arms in prayer to support just causes and those who rule justly (Origen). Consequently, nationalistic appurtenances are relativized. Christian communities fight against their home governments when these sow terror elsewhere. The production and sale of arms to countries which receive foreign aid to feed their starving millions, the positioning of colonial armies in Africa by France, the support of dictators like Mobutu, Eyadema, and their ilk by the West, and so on, are all causes of bloodshed produced by Christians against Christians. No Christian church should remain indifferent before this denial of humanity to Africans and indeed to two-thirds of the world's poor. Western democratic governments should be made to abandon the unhappy history of protecting the bourgeoisie at home and helping to destroy the structures of weaker societies.

The metaphor of church as family of God introduces warmth and caring as the controlling principles of our fellowship. "Christ has come to restore the world to unity, a single human Family in the image of the trinitarian Family. We are the Family of God: this is the Good News! The same blood flows in our veins, and it is the blood of Jesus

Christ."[13] The churches and other nongovernmental organizations are already active in giving help to war victims in Rwanda, Somalia, Liberia, and Angola; victims of the devaluation of the CFA francs are given temporary reprieve in various French cities by Caritas and other church organizations; political refugees are helped to process their papers. These aids are important. But the most effective and important aid is the aid to put an end to all begging, to all misery, to all oppression. It involves a gigantic new wave of evangelization to mobilize the conscience of the West, to mobilize Africans and all human beings, for the defense of Africans whose very survival on planet earth is as much threatened today as was the case with Amerindians and the blacks of Australia.

Sharing with the West the Basics of the African Notion of Person

The new wave of evangelization, which involves the promotion of humane living in Africa and the world, will benefit from sharing with the West and the world community the core elements of the African relational notion of person. Far from dissolving individuality, it promotes individual gifts for the benefit of the community. "A person is a person because others are." In *Habits of the Heart*, Bellah and his colleagues have pointed out the hollowness of the person which is created by radical American individualism. To avoid the empty self and empty relationships, which are the results of the theory of the absolutely free self and contractual relationships, therapists advise their clients to reconnect to families, join churches, or be involved in political activity.[14] Despite the individualism of America, it is a country very well known for favoring a multiplicity of associations. There is an evident hunger for the traditional patterns of warmth, caring, and closeness despite the fear of commitment. The empty self of radical individualism exists only in theory.

The solidarity between churches in the experience of the new family of God, based on autonomy and communion, should be translated into the sharing of sustainable human values. Solidarity should no longer be restricted to the sharing of personnel or to financial aid. It is not simply an issue of benefactor and beneficiary churches. Cultural treasures, especially spiritual treasures of humane living, of interconnections between humans and the environment, are indispensable for the reconstruction of society. Both the community and the individual are subjects of right. The autonomy of the individual is realized in relationship and is directed towards the construction of a more humane society. Human freedom or autonomy is not simply to protect the limited interest of the individual person, even if no harm is done to the other, as utilitarian and expressive individualism defends. Freedom should be experienced and expressed in creative dimensions—the freedom to create a better society. Consequently, freedom should not be understood simply in terms of personal economic interest because such a definition would exclude those who are not economically self-reliant from its enjoyment. It will be understood principally in terms of creating a more caring human community, a caring which is certainly enhanced by economic advancement.

The emphasis on this relational dimension of the person may be a way of insisting on the corporate responsibility of companies for the harm they do elsewhere in the world in the free pursuit of their interests; it may be a way of showing Western societies and the world at large their corporate responsibility for the evils produced by communities and technologies. It may form the basis for the reconciliation of the various human societies and races. It may be the basis for discussing the reconciliation between Africa and West.

Slavery: Compensation and Reconciliation

The year 1992 marked the 500-year anniversary of the European invasion of the Americas. In that year the world remembered the beginning of the ineluctable drawing of the rest of the human race into the orbit of Western influence. There were many ways of saluting that phenomenal achievement. There was naturally high esteem for the courage and prowess of Columbus and his crew. But there were also bitter memories of the nearly liquidated Amerindians and the enslaved blacks. Let me repeat, conquests are not new in the turbulent history of humankind. Slavery is an old institution, practiced among Africans before the modern period. But what was new was the planned eradication of a people because they belonged to a different race. What was new was the denial of the humanity of enslaved peoples because they were of a different color. Such an action was planned and executed by human groups which called themselves Christian. Today the decimated and discriminated groups form part of this new people of God. Consequently, it becomes inevitable that reflection on the interrelationship within the new family of God, as the sign or sacrament of relationship in the larger world, must lead to one kind of reconciliation or another.

Some in Africa, especially in Nigeria, have called for compensation or reparation to be made to Africa for the enslavement of her sons and daughters. Oftentimes such calls do not pay close attention to the criminal collusion of African leaders, between the fifteenth and the ninteenth centuries, in the slave trade. I have examined local African participation in slavery and the impact this has had on the material and spiritual history of Africa. As I noted above, such an exercise in "dangerous remembering" will ensure that the evils of the past will not be repeated. It will ensure also that wherever the humanity of the black race or any other persecuted group of people is denied, one should not rest until such racism is removed. But this is exactly what has not been wiped out from the practice of our time.

From the time Bartolomé de Las Casas requested the transportation of enslaved Africans to the Americas to the present day, the black race has been dehumanized and deprived of its rights. The famous words of the American Declaration of Independence, drafted by Thomas Jefferson, that "all men are created equal" was proclaimed and implemented in an America of the eighteenth century which did not consider the enslaved blacks among the human species. Even after two centuries of struggle the rights of black Americans are still mostly on paper. Freedom in America is too closely tied up with economic success; and the greater percentage of the black population is far removed from the successful American middle class. The massive increase in xenophobia all over Europe, especially in these days of economic recession, has blacks as special targets. I am in no way suggesting that blacks are little angels. I am not saying that some are not involved in breaking immigration laws, in selling drugs, and so on. I am only insisting that the white race targets blacks more easily for discrimination because of their color. They are targeted because of the history of slavery and colonialism. They are doubly targeted because of the weakness of their home economies. Poverty is experienced on a double track: material poverty and anthropological poverty.

What contribution has the community called church, which experiences warmth and caring as the family of God, to make in such a situation of gross discrimination? It is here, I think, that the two concepts of compensation and reconciliation should be explored very lucidly for the healing of relationship among humans, for the re-creation of the world.

Compensation is paid to a wronged party. But before such a debt is paid, the guilty party must admit guilt. "Christian Europe" and "Puritan America" did not think they were doing any wrong to Africans by enslaving them. Rather, Christian Europe believed that by enslaving the blacks they were snatching their souls from the clutches of Satan. And since Europe and America benefitted from the labor of the brutalized African bodies, there were no losers. The slave was blessed with salvation outside this world, and the slave master reaped divine blessings in economic progress. And for "Puritan America" the black slave was a property bought with hard-earned money. It is true that the Roman popes went back on earlier decisions of their predecessors to condemn slavery. It is also true that the issue came before Vatican I. One must laud the struggles of humanists and church people such as William Wilberforce to put an end to slavery. But the practice was stopped more because slavery was no longer economically viable than because it denied the humanity of Africans. It is at this level that Europe and America must admit guilt—the denial of the humanity of Africans because of the color of their skin. It is precisely because this guilt was not publicly admitted, and because compensation was not paid for the evil, that the enslavement of Africa continues unchallenged and takes on a more sophisticated face. Africa's problem today is "their" problem; it is not the problem of the human race. If the sons and daughters of Europe and America realize that the foundation of the fortunes they are sitting on was built on the hecatombs of children, young women, and men, torn from their homeland, they will reflect before claiming that the crisis of Africa is not their concern.

Once again let me make myself clear. I am in no way minimizing the responsibility of Africans for the crisis in our cultural, political, economic, and social life. But I want to insist that it is not simple rhetoric to make claims for compensation. The idea of compensation arising from the admission of guilt is closely linked with reconciliation.

There were many important celebrations in Western Europe in the year 1994. The most important celebration was the Allied landing in Normandy fifty years earlier; a landing which signalled the beginning of the end of the Second World War. The memory of the landing, celebrated with all fanfare, was not supposed to rekindle old hates or to humiliate conquered Germany, even though Germany was not invited to the celebration. The memory was to ensure that an evil of such magnitude not be repeated. During the series of celebrations, Germany, which has been in the forefront of the construction of the European Union, made a significant gesture of compensation and reconciliation. The German chancellor, Helmut Kohl, ceremonially returned scores of painting which were forcibly removed from French families during the German occupation. This is not only a sign of genuine national admission of guilt; it is also a sign of the move towards new relationships. Reconciliation is not possible without the admission of guilt. One may compare this gesture of the German people with the snubbing of Africans by the British Museum in 1976 when it refused to return, or at least lend, to Nigeria the Benin Mask, which was chosen as the symbol of the 1977 Black Festival of Arts and Culture held in Lagos. The prevalent British logic was that weather conditions were unfavorable to ensure the preservation of the mask, a work of art stolen from Benin City during the colonial period!

Europe has not admitted guilt in the enslavement and colonization of Africa. In the European psyche, those adventures in such dangerous circumstances were a help to civilize the black race. Africans should, rather, keep on thanking Europe for the benefits of the encounter. I can only say that this kind of evil will keep on begetting other evils like Auschwitz and Rwanda until the guilt for the denial of the humanity of the black race is fully admitted. The history of humanity has never witnessed such physical, cultural, political, economic, and religious destruction. No such plunder has ever been witnessed. The history of humanity has not known such a collaboration between religious and political institutions to theorize and execute such dehumanization. John Paul II's admission of guilt and request for pardon in favor of Europe is only the symbolic beginning of a new relationship. In the context of a church which is becoming more and more centralized and is not too anxious to put behind her the colonial pattern of relationship with Africa, it may also mark the beginning of the decolonization of the church.

Before the Special Assembly of the Synod of Bishops for Africa, the European members of "Initiative Kindugu" (a Swahili word meaning fraternity), signed a document in which they addressed the issue of the admission of guilt. Among those who appended their signatures were bishops, medical doctors, family fathers and mothers, missionaries, professors, artists, journalists, members of organizations such as Missio, Misereor, Lenten Fund, and so on. The tone of the document shows that the confession of guilt aims to build a new kind of relationship:

> We Christian men and women from Europe, gathered in INITIA-TIVE KINDUGU, salute the entire Church of Africa on the occasion of your Synod 1994. . . . As Europeans we have reason to turn to you: In grief and pain we acknowledge the countless wrongs inflicted on African people. We are ready to identify ourselves with the sins of our ancestors. We have begun to examine the ways in which we ourselves up to this day have part in the oppression of and contempt for your dignity and self-determination, politically, economically, ecologically, culturally and even ecclesiologically. We confess having both individually and communually [sic] contributed in various ways to existing social structures as well as to ecclesial paternalism. We regret not always having played our part to undo such injustice. It seems impossible to assess the extent of such sin or even to redress it. We dare ask for forgiveness of yourselves and of your ancestors only before God and his son Jesus Christ who reconciled us to Himself and to one another through His own suffering and death. We are resolved never to let the memory of our wrongdoings fade but to strive for conversion with courage and self-denial. God alone can bring about the healing. With you we beseech Him for it.[15]

Such initiatives by the bishop of Rome and by Christian groups like Initiative Kindugu should constitute patterns of mounting pressure on the consciences of Europe and America to admit their guilt and show signs of readiness for reconciliation. As the Germans returned the stolen French works of art, so should London, Paris, Bonn, and other cities start thinking of showing signs of genuine repentance by returning stolen African works of art or paying for them and making reparations for the evils committed in Africa through slavery and colonialism.

The Bishops' Call for the Cancellation of Africa's Debts: An Ethical Issue

It is under the rubric of compensation and reconciliation that one should revisit the urgent call by the synod Fathers in the Special Assembly for Africa for the cancellation of the debts owed the Western finance houses by Africa. Kamgang has argued in his book *Au delà de la conférence nationale* that, as a matter of honor, the debts must be repaid. But, of course, he foresees the departure of the present breed of unimaginative rulers, whose continued stay in power is an obstacle to the progress of Africa, before considering the repayment of such debts. It is from the ethical point of view that thirty-seven bishops, coming from all parts of Africa, during the synod (April 1994) signed an "Open Letter" calling on their brother bishops of Europe and America to prevail on their home governments to cancel the debts.

"The Open Letter from the Bishops of Africa to Our Brother Bishops in Europe and North America" drew attention to the fact that the debt is unpayable because of the poverty of Africa. It also drew attention to the ethical issue: it is morally wrong to deprive a nation of the means to meet the basic needs of its people in order to repay debt; the needs of the poor take precedence over the wants of the rich. In the context of the church as family of God, in the warmth and caring which should prevail in the relationship of *agape* between the churches, the bishops called for concerted action of witness both in Africa and in Europe and America.

The right of the Church to intervene in political and economic affairs is limited in any part of the Church. Yet the social teaching of the Church is part of her mandate to go and teach all nations. These are times when justice compels us to speak publicly on these matters. If we remain silent and inactive, whether in Africa or the countries of the North, we may appear as cowards or accomplices rather than as champions of justice. We have the right and duty to enlighten the consciences of the decision makers. The question of African debt offers an opportunity for the Bishops of Africa to work in partnership with their fellow bishops in Europe and America to seek a just and speedy way of resolving it. For our part in Africa, we pledge ourselves to address the internal factors that contribute to the debt crisis. The Church in Africa has always been a fearless champion of human rights and democracy; we reaffirm our resolve to continue to use non-violent ways to overcome corruption, oppression and economic mismanagement among our government officials, military and ruling elite. We ask our sister Churches in Europe and America to help to bring about a swift and just resolution of our problem of unpayable debts. This is inextricably linked with unjust conditions of world trade where the price of our commodities has collapsed to an all time low. It is also related to the urgent need for reform of the Structural Adjustment Programmes which cause great suffering among the poor.[16]

The view of the bishops that the church constitutes an alternative society to challenge the unjust and unethical programs of the International Monetary Fund (IMF) and the World Bank should not pass unnoticed. The church-family, spread out through the world, at the service of the Kingdom, guided by the Spirit of Jesus, plays the prophetic role of defending the poor against the pretensions of the rich, of creating an ecology for the easy implantation of the Kingdom. Theology and ethics can no longer pretend that questions of development, economy, and ecology are not primary concerns.

The religious dimension of the program and discourse of the IMF and the World Bank is a matter for concern and should not go unchallenged. Mihevc has drawn attention to what he calls the "fundamentalist theology of the World Bank." In a lucid analysis he shows that this "theology" consists of an agenda and a discourse that not only denies the legitimacy of alternatives but ensures that all of the options available to developing countries have been narrowed down to one. This one option, Structural Adjustment Programs (SAPs), is community-destroying and death-dealing. Imbued with a dangerously religious and messianic fervor and replacing the missionaries, economists of the World Bank peddle the "open market economy" and the Bank's ideology of development as natural law.[17] What emerges from this program is protecting religiously the particular American notion of the individual which I have described above—the middle-class individual who should be allowed to have access to all markets and to take advantage of the weaker economies of the world. The World Bank confessed indirectly its failure to lead Africa into the Eden of success when it admitted that the stronger African economies following its programs will not get out of the poverty line in the next twenty years. From the devastating effects of IMF and World Bank programs in Africa and the Third World, especially beginning in the 1980s, development issues must never again be withdrawn from the cultural, religious, political, economic, ecological, and theological domains. So much is clear from the intervention of Catholic bishops at the Synod for Africa and their plea for the forgiveness of the debts.

With the fiftieth anniversary of the establishment of the World Bank and IMF at Bretton Woods (July 1944-1994), there has been a concerted action by church organizations and NGOs to say clearly that enough is enough. According to the London-based Catholic Institute for International Relations, "The 'Fifty Years Is Enough' campaign, a growing coalition of more than one hundred development groups worldwide, has called for the IMF and World Bank to be denied further funds until reforms are introduced to make them socially accountable."[18] The role of these bodies in the recolonization of Africa, coupled with the unfair trade agreements of GATT and the World Trade Organization, leaves the impression that the predatory attitude of the West toward Africa has not changed. How else does one explain the attitude of these organizations, established by the United States and Britain to rebuild the world financial system and international trade after the Second World War, in prescribing such death-dealing pills for Africa? For the creation of a humane order in the world with human life as priority, the focus of the prayer of our thirty-seven bishops should shift from the forgiveness of African debts to the payment of the debt owed Africa. This must be seen as the viable basis for reconciliation.

Reconciliation as Binding Life Together—an Igbo Paradigm

The churches of the West and Africa should undertake their mediatory ministry of reconciliation first and foremost as one united and reconciled body. Maintaining its local autonomy but intimately linked by communion, the church-family needs to be experienced in our world as a challenging and prophetic family. This activity should not be limited to declarations; there must be commitment to action.

The Igbo people of Nigeria have a cultural-religious practice of frequently renewing relationships which are endangered by well-known human limitations. Marriage in crisis and relationships between families, business associates, clans, and village-groups are ritually renewed when endangered by betrayal or failure. The ritual for this renewal is called *igba ndu* (binding life together, or making a covenant). God, ancestors, divinities (especially the powerful Earth Spirit), and the entire community act together in the rite to re-create the society. The terms for renewal are spelled out. The participants call on all the divinities to bear united witness of their commitment to the life-enhancing terms of behavior. This ritual has been Christianized and has been yielding interesting results in the healing and renewal of relationships of all types.

The jungle, which is our world of today, needs such a reconciliation to heal and renew relationships. The contemporary world of politics and economy is built principally on the predominant modern Western "civilizational" model (Maurier), which is utilitarian individualism. This has created the situation where four-fifths of humankind live in terrible poverty. According to one U.S. analyst, the poor live in "homelands" remote from the rich, migration on any large scale is impermissible, no systematic redistribution of income exists, and the rich enjoy a decisive military superiority and engage in frequent interventions against the poor countries. This is the destructive victory of radical individualism.

In fairness, Western governments are not comfortable with this situation. They, however, lack the political will and the spiritual stamina to attempt other viable alternatives. It is not easy for change to be effected by the impersonal transnational corporations or the governments run by a bureaucracy. In my view change must begin in the assembly which calls itself the family of God. It is a change which involves commitment. The action programs which follow declarations and commitments by our churches and other NGOs should already indicate the determination to establish dynamic patterns of humane living in the relationship between peoples in our world.

The church as family of God calls for warmth and sharing, and especially for a lucid analysis of the crisis which converts life in our world into hell. It involves a radical reexamination of our failures and an evaluation of ways and means to reestablish humane living in our planet. The human traditions of Africa and the world community and the prophetic challenge of the life of the risen Jesus form the basis for this reconstruction. But the starting point for the church in Africa to join in the reconstruction of Africa and to convincingly play a mediatory role in the reconciliation of peoples is self-reliance. The African church must demonstrate its ability to stand on its own feet to challenge the very structures of dependency, which are the bane of life on the continent.

Putting an End to the African Church's Dependency Syndrome

The open letter of the African bishops to their brother bishops in Europe and America demonstrates the necessary interdependence in resolving world problems in order to bear witness to the Reign of God. The forthright language of the African bishops in the 1994 synod demonstrates a necessary responsibility for the life of the church in its witness on the continent. The metaphor of the church-family, related to the Trinitarian family, ties together the autonomy and communion which characterize life in the assembly of God's people. The close link which we have shown existed between enslavement, colonization, and the church makes it imperative that the prevailing mentality of recolonization and enslavement of African peoples should be clearly resisted in the church. Colonization and enslavement are more potent when they are sacralized. The church in Africa must show herself capable of being fully decolonized in order to see, judge, and act in favor of the liberation of the African poor. In order to do this, our churches must depend on their own spiritual and material resources. These constitute the local resources brought into the communion of churches. While it may be easy to clearly pinpoint the dimensions of the spiritual resources of the African church, the material resources are more difficult to locate. Indeed, the dependency syndrome of the churches in Africa on the material level appears to be congenital. Material dependency leaves the road wide open to lack of creativity and even blackmail. Solidarity, mutuality, partnership, sharing, and interdependence among the churches are current concepts in describing the terms of communion among the churches. But the beggar has no self-respect. Self-respect for the churches of Africa, and indeed for the African nations, will keep on being elusive until there is a certain level of self-reliance on the material level.

The Need to Reexamine the Question of Foreign Aid

As I said about foreign aid to our destroyed economies, I want to state clearly that the type of foreign aid that the church in Africa is currently receiving may not be in the best interests of Africa. This assertion may appear grossly irresponsible. Think of the hunger in Sudan, Somalia, and Ethiopia; think of the human tragedy in Rwanda and the refugee situation in Zaire, Tanzania, and Angola; think of the great risks for NGOs and especially church organizations like Caritas. How does one justify such an irresponsible statement? I have already discussed above the root causes of these evils and how relationships in the church-family will be translated into an efficient networking to attack the problems at their sources. Confronted by the impersonal, faceless, ubiquitous, and exploitative capitalist system, the churches and NGOs are powerless. They spend themselves and their resources in providing temporary relief to the suffering masses. But their "ambulance ministry" affords only a temporary reprieve. A more fundamental action program would go to the root causes of the crisis. It finds out where the gas is leaking, where there is a short-circuit, in order to put an end to all "fire fighting." This involves an objective analysis of the relevant contexts of the continent (or countries), shedding the light of the gospel on those situations and drawing lucid principles of reflection, norms of judgment, and directives for action from the social teachings of the church.[19]

The question of putting an end to all foreign aid in the church is not new. Twenty years ago (1974), the Protestant All Africa Conference of Churches (AACC) called for a moratorium on the sending of foreign missionaries and foreign aid. The AACC was convinced that the church in Africa would not be truly local until it enjoyed autonomy, responsibility, and self-reliance. Or, in the language of the Association of the Member Episcopal Conferences of Eastern Africa (AMECEA), the "localization" of the church must be understood in terms of a self-supporting, self-ministering, and self-propagating church-community. Catholics and Protestants would thus applaud the vision of the AACC. However, the AACC's interpretation of the continued missionary presence in Africa and the flow of missionary aid as harmful to the realization of these noble objectives was clearly rejected by the Catholic church leadership and by many national conferences of the Protestant church groups.[20]

The reaction of the Catholic bishops was speedy and nuanced. The 1974 synod on evangelization was a very important occasion for the participating bishops to make a pronouncement which represented the viewpoint of the Catholic church leadership in Africa. Bishop Zoa of

Yaoundé, Cameroon, spoke for the other bishops. His declaration was prefaced by a refutation of certain radical positions adopted by the review *Spiritus* on the issue of the moratorium. F. Eboussi Boulaga, in the said review, expressed his view in an article entitled "La démission" (Resignation). His conclusion was that the missionaries should plan their departure in an orderly way, so that the African church leadership might fully take over in order to determine the direction of evangelization on the continent.[21]

The response of the bishops positively underlined the importance of communion, partnership, coresponsibility, and interdependence in the relationship with the sister churches of the West and the missionary congregations. The bishops rejected the moratorium but they did not reject the arguments for autonomy. They supported the need for incarnational theological research in Africa; and they insisted that the missionaries should make themselves available to the local churches but refrain from dictating to the churches.

The bishops' position doused the fears of the missionaries and consoled the bishops themselves. It was a reassuring position. As Bishop Patrick Kalilombe cleverly put it, it is like eating one's cake and still having it. You enjoy autonomy and foreign aid at the same time. You are liberated from slavery with the resources of the slave master.

But the bishops did not really have any option. The 1974 statistics and the 1994 figures will convince any doubting Thomases that the major victims (or beneficiaries) of foreign aid to the churches in Africa are bishops, priests, religious women and men, and seminarians. These are uppermost in the minds of the bishops whenever they leave Africa, cap in hand, for Europe and America to look for aid to run the churches. The needs of catechists, Catholic hospitals, Catholic education (as distinct from seminary training), and charity to the poor come after the major needs of the clerical class.

In his report to the 1994 synod before the interventions ("Relatio ante disceptationem") the chief reporter (Cardinal Hyacinthe Thiandoum of Dakar, Senegal) touched briefly on the question of the recruitment, training, and adequate maintenance of all church personnel. What he said is of interest to our present discussion.

The church in Africa is poor mainly because Africa is poor. But heavy and continued dependence on foreign financial sources of aid should be a cause for major concern. Certainly we appreciate and are grateful for the Christian solidarity and charity of our richer and older Churches who have been coming to our aid. But we too must play our role in seeking ways of greater self-reliance.[22]

The matter can be stated in this way without betraying the thought of the cardinal: "The poverty-stricken church in a poor Africa is first preoccupied with the adequate maintenance of her clergy"! However, it is a very well-known fact that with foreign aid the clergy has been more than adequately maintained, as the cardinal indirectly indicated in an earlier reference to the highly respected priests.

> The priest must not fail to live up to this dignity. At the same time, however, the priest in Africa today must define his image in terms of collaboration with the whole People of God, and in solidarity with the real living conditions of the people at large. It would be a pity if he were to become part of the small cream of affluent elite in a sea of misery (No. 9).

The crucial issue is whether one needs aid for such able-bodied, healthy victims of charity. Do we need aid for the clerical class? How can the church in Africa avoid the alienation that goes along with receiving without giving? As leaders of a church which must be prophetic, which must witness to the Kingdom within the local context and in the pluralistic international context and exercise communion with sister churches, how can the clergy see, judge, and act with responsibility when a lot of the time they are thinking about the views of the donor churches? Can the church leadership avoid the temptation of responding to the wishes of those who pay the piper? Is the church in Africa ready to muster the courage to challenge the politics and economics of the stomach in the communion of churches? Is it possible to avoid the temptation to think that relationship with the donor churches is more important than relationship with sister churches of the national and continental conferences? Is it possible to justify on the basis of the gospel *agape* the continued reception of this kind of help to support a privileged clerical class?

The African Clergy Should Guide the African World
into Self-Reliance

In a recent book, *Les missions*, French anthropologist and missiologist Henri Maurier made a spirited defense of the role of European missionaries in "universalizing" Western civilization. In his materialist (or anthropological) approach, Maurier attached great importance to two concepts—"civilizational" and "universalizing." "Civilizational" embraces the technological know-how, arts and artifacts, writing, systems of government, and religious systems which produce a particular social group and keeps that group together. "Universalizing" embraces the successful enterprise of uniting various social groups to share a particular "civilizational" model instead of remaining isolated, autonomous, and self-sufficient. Missionaries were the principal agents of promoting the dominant Western "civilizational" pattern whether they liked it or not.

Maurier has a very illuminating paragraph on vocations to the priesthood, religious life, celibacy, and so on. He makes a very interesting point about the type of sociocultural conditions which favor such vocations. People called to these vocations are freed by society from providing for their daily subsistence; and this involves a considerable financial outlay. For the success of the Christian "missions," according to Maurier, it is evident that "dependency on the dominant civilizational order" must totally prevail. A society must produce sufficient surplus in order to liberate such personnel for purely religious functions. Consequently, not all human societies have the adequate "civilizational development" to set aside such personnel and furnish them with all their needs. For example, one of the principal reasons for the collapse of the church in the Kongo kingdom (sixteenth and seventeenth centuries) was the inability of the Kongo "civilizational development" to maintain the clergy. "Evidently, the Congolese civilization was incapable of supporting the burden of such a complex clerical structure."[23] For the sake of argument, is the African civilization today capable of sustaining a complex Western clerical structure? Should the support of such a clerical structure be the priority of the church in Africa?

Maurier's book is written at the end of the twentieth century to justify "missions" by appealing to those very points of reproach which

Western missionaries prefer not to talk about—the involvement of missionaries in slavery, colonization, the propagation of Western civilization, the neocolonization of Africa, and so on. Instead of pointing to the destructiveness of Western civilization, one should, rather, note in anthropological terms, according to Maurier, the ineluctability of such destructions and the positive consequences (civilizational and universalizing) such destructions bring to humankind. His materialist interpretation of the work of missionaries does not admit of euphemisms. The emergence of the local clergy may indicate the maturity of a church but not its independence from the Roman "imperial, monarchical, centralizing authority"; such a pyramidal command structure forms part of the administrative apparatus of "universalizing" religions. Needless to say, autonomy and self-reliance are excluded.

Many who may not accept Maurier's reductionist interpretation of "missions" may share his view on the dependency of the rest of the world church on the Western "civilizational" pattern of maintaining a clerical class. The facts are that this dominant pattern has been the practice. And insofar as the present structures of ministry in the church are maintained, one does not foresee any change. And to continue to maintain such structures would mean, according to Kalilombe, that there will be no self-reliant church in Africa.

We shall not of course succumb to this ideological and monocultural interpretation of the church despite the fact that it has been the prevalent model for many centuries. It is this image which led, in the first place, to the AACC's call for the moratorium twenty years ago. The then general secretary of the AACC, Canon Burgess Carr, was credited to have said, "Should the moratorium cause missionary-sending agencies to crumble, the African church would have performed a service in redeeming God's people in the Northern Hemisphere from a distorted view of the mission of the Church in the world."[24]

It is true that today vocations are crippled in the West. But the shift to the Third World—Indonesia, India, Tanzania, Nigeria—has been effectively maintained, thanks to the financial resources of the West. The increase in vocations, instead of representing the autonomy and self-reliance of the African church, rather entrenches dependency. This dependency is deeply rooted because of an extroverted church, because of the persistence of the colonial model of the church. From the ring to the sock, the African bishop must be a reproduction of his Western counterpart. And having adequately maintained the agents of evangelization, one must find the means to support the visible signs of successful evangelization in Western terms (hospitals, orphanages, schools, and so on). To add insult to injury, dying congregations in the West invade African cities, uninvited, to recruit African candidates. Money, the magic sign of freedom and success, can buy African vocations to service the aged sisters and brothers of these congregations. The practice is spreading with such rapidity that the Fathers in the just concluded African synod were constrained to cry out against such a warped definition of being church. Such institutes which do not have houses in Africa, according to the synod Fathers, should not come seeking for new vocations without prior dialogue with the local ordinary.[25]

One faith, one hope, one baptism! How could we justify the reduction of these marks of the church to visible structures and especially to the establishment of a privileged class? In a continent of hunger, a continent that some have characterized, in the words of Fidel Castro, as "a nonworld," does the church leadership feel no evangelical and moral revulsion at being presented as "part of the small cream of affluent elite in a sea of misery"? In a continent where efficient experts are a luxury, why should a group of highly intelligent, disciplined, and committed young women and men be set aside to live off the labor of others? Is it not possible to mobilize these able-bodied, intelligent, disciplined, and generous young Africans for a ministry which sees the coming of the Reign of God in holistic terms—already present in the lifestyle of the assembly in this world and to be fully realized in the next?

Let us use Nigeria as an example. The seminaries are overflowing. The bishops' conference created more major seminaries in order to limit the intake to a maximum of 350 students. This control has been very difficult to implement. With the exception of three major seminaries belonging to religious congregations, the other seven major seminaries always number over 350. The three seminaries in eastern Nigeria, led by Bigard Memorial Seminary Enugu, have no less than 500 candidates each. Entry requirements are very high, with the same academic requirements as Nigerian universities (most of the seminaries are either affiliated with the universities or are seeking such an affiliation). Other requirements include good health, moral discipline, and prayer life. In 1992 the vocations director of the Spiritans (Holy Ghost Fathers and Brothers of Nigeria) received 200 applications. After a process of elimination he called about 50 candidates for interviews. I was one of the interviewers. From the 50 we were to select 15 candidates for the postulancy. The criteria for selection included an articulation of missionary interest, academic qualifications, age (younger people are preferred), involvement in society and church, catchment (ethnic) area (non-Igbo candidates are favored), and so on. The cream of Nigerian youth is chosen to be made priests or religious. Their peers enter universities or learn a trade. They struggle to get one meal a day unless they are the children of the elite. But our seminarians are assured of three meals a day and of all the educational facilities at the undergraduate level. The greater percentage of the subsidy comes from overseas. Sometimes major seminaries have closed in Nigeria because these monies were not forthcoming.

The average Nigerian young woman or man must undergo severe trials to succeed in life. They struggle, economize, cheat, take jobs, push drugs, practice prostitution in order to get through four years of university education. Our seminarians go through eight years of philosophical and theological training with little concern for their basic livelihood. Parents, relations, friends, Christian mothers, and wealthy Christians assure that they are clothed and have pocket money. The bishops and Rome ensure their feeding and seminary education. They are trained from day one to be dependent: able-bodied, intelligent, committed, and drawn from the cream of the society but dependent and shielded from the major crises experienced by the average African youth! After ordination they depend on the bishop for assignment.

Clerical Dependency as a System of Control

The dependency means first and foremost *control*. The control is rooted in the most elemental or primitive human preoccupation, *the stomach*. Rarely does one bite the finger that provides the nourishment. And rarely is the complaint of one who is so fed and whose pocket money is provided taken seriously. Thus the agents of evangelization may have plenty, but their human rights are far from being fully assured. A beggar has no choice.

In Nigeria, especially among the Igbo, an apprentice spends five to seven years training under a mentor. After that he or she begins an independent trade. The mentor provides a lump sum of money or procures major equipment which will ensure the independence of the apprentice to face the world as an adult. Today this is still the most popular way of making one's way in the world. The dependency is temporary. If one fails, one has only one's self to blame. This pattern of cooperation is entrenched in Igbo and other Nigerian cultures. In the eighteenth-century autobiography of Olaudah Equiano, an Igbo who was sold into slavery and won his freedom in Great Britain, Equiano clearly underlined that among his people there were no beggars. Up to the Nigeria-Biafra war and after, the Igbo culture would not tolerate begging. Even handicapped people such as the blind and the lame always learned a trade in order to escape the shame and humiliation that go with dependency. When doing social work among refugees in Ihiala during that terrible war (1967-1970), I saw the wisdom in the decision of some Spiritans (such as James McNulty) in trying to save the face of displaced people who were constrained to beg. They were given jobs such as cultivating all available land—football fields, tennis courts, and so on. In that way they received aid with dignity. The Marist Brothers of the School created "Hopeville" in Uturu (Imo State) after the civil war to rehabilitate the handicapped victims of the war. These were taught various trades to help them reintegrate into the society. Even the community of resettled ex-lepers administered by the Marist Brothers in Enugu insist on self-reliance by cultivating their land and learning crafts such as making cane chairs in order to provide for most of their needs. And yet we assemble able-bodied, intelligent, disciplined, and committed young women and men and make them dependent!

Dependency in the church has become a system of social control. These young women and men could provide for their livelihood, like their peers who did not choose the priestly or religious vocation, if self-reliance were integrated into their formation. But dependency makes subservience or "obedience" the first law in the administration of the church. It ensures the pyramidal command structure of the church. The person who has the purse calls all the shots. Keeping the purse and making sure that it is always full becomes the principal occupation of the bishop or the religious superior. He or she must learn the new ways of telling the story of the diocese or congregation according to the handbook on aid or begging; the kind of maps and pictures to send to the donor agencies; the angle of African life to emphasize—the more one stresses poverty and misery the more hope one has to get aid. In this way a warped view of life in Africa is created. (The haven or oasis of the elite, along with their overseas connections, which produce the poor conditions in Africa never show as part of the story of Africa.) Our church leaders go through humiliations and controls by Roman agencies and donor agencies in order to get the funds to maintain themselves and their coworkers. Just as the priest or seminarian will couch criticisms of the bishop and his manner of administration in euphemisms, so the bishop will be wary about what kind of comments to make about Rome or the agencies which provide for his diocese. A diocesan priest from one African country has remarked how familiar and simple our bishops appear when they visit Europe. The student-priests become their brothers. But as soon as they get back to Africa, the hierarchical lines once again become firmly drawn. Does it need much imagination to divine that in Europe the beggar-bishop is reduced to the masses? Back home, with his purse filled, he calls the shots as usual.

We must get out of this quagmire! The Western "civilizational" model of ministry in the church is a model of the Western patriarchate. "Universalized" as it is by Western missionaries, no one should pretend that it is "universal." We must get out of the dependency syndrome! And we have the means to do so. "What resources do we dispose of?" queries Cardinal Thiandoum in his opening report to the African synod. "The most important, after the grace of Christ, is the People. The whole People of God . . . has the mandate, which is both an honor and a duty, to proclaim the Gospel message" (no. 8). We must move beyond the making of material or economic success—as decreed by utilitarian individualism—the visible sign of success or enjoyment of freedom in the world. The church as family of God must first assert its independence of this creeping materialism, which is the root cause of the humiliations of Africans irrespective of whether they are leaders of our churches or of our states. The motivation and the mobilization of the whole People of God on the continent to fight the poverty and oppression must start with dismantling the bourgeois clericalism which has been the legacy of the Western church. *The church in Africa does not need any foreign aid to support a clerical class.* While thanking our sister churches of Europe and America for their generosity, we join the Episcopal Conference of Zaire and the just concluded Synod for Africa to state clearly that "our Churches should take responsibility for themselves." And according to Bishop Kembo Mamputu of Matadi, Zaire, the reasons are methodological and pastoral, ecclesiological and soteriological in nature, since our populations continue in poverty and misery. "If our ecclesial communities remain eternally beggars, how can they contribute to the sociocultural development of our society and help the faithful to build their own city?"[26] There must be a fundamental shift in the notion of ministry in the church of Christ in Africa.

Reeducating Priests and Religious

Instead of plunging Africa deeper and deeper into dependency, those called to priestly and religious vocations must be educated to lead the continent back to her lost dignity. In the West the clergy had not always depended on the charity of the laity. The mobilization of medieval Europe to convert areas of brushwood and swamp into arable land, to clear forests and drain swamps, was led by the monasteries. According to Paul Johnson, "bishoprics and abbacies constituted the core of the agricultural economy of Europe." The heritage from Benedict (and also Columbanus) popularized *manual labor* as part of the daily occupation of the monk (and not something reserved to the slave). Of particular interest were the Cistercian monks who came on the scene from the end of the eleventh century. Intelligent, drawn from the families of the elite, disciplined, highly organized, uncompromising, and ruthless, they "became the agricultural apostles of Europe's internal colonization." Disposing of the peasantry, as Benedictines disposed of slave labor, because it was economically unprofitable, the Cistercians recruited large numbers of landless and workless youth, turned them into lay brothers (bound by the three vows but unable to become priests), and welded them into a highly disciplined and motivated labor force. From Portugal to Sweden, Scotland to Hungary, each of the 742 Cistercian monasteries had huge flourishing farms.[27]

One cannot accept without criticism Maurier's thesis of a Western "civilizational" model that set aside a clerical class totally maintained by tithes. It has to be put in the perspective of the contribution of the church to the development of Europe and to her role in the struggle against misery and poverty. The story of the development of agriculture in Europe and the creation of a powerful Europe cannot be fully told without the managerial competence of the monasteries.

We do not have to employ the feudalistic methods of the medieval church in order to make the clergy contribute to the eradication of misery on the continent. But our intelligent, committed, disciplined young women and men need only to be rightly motivated and challenged in order to embrace a pattern of holistic evangelization which rejects the blasphemous distinction between the material and the spiritual, the separation of the economic and political from the domains of religion and theology. The canonical prescription which forbids the clergy from engaging in business may have increased the irresponsibility of this class in its use of material goods.

Bishops, priests, and laypeople who intervened in the African Synod called for a renewal of priestly formation. Seminary formation, as recommended in the final submissions of the synod, must ensure that our seminarians are fully in touch with the social, political, and economic realities of the African context. Bishop Vandame of N'djaména (Chad), who bemoaned the fact that his diocese is "maintained intravenously," regretted that living by foreign donations made his priests lose a sense of reality: they no longer saw money as a result of work but as an abstract value which must always be there. He called for the training of seminarians in bookkeeping and the training of laypeople in the Yaoundé Business Management School of the Catholic University of Yaoundé (Cameroon) to help in the responsible administration of church property.[28]

The Luba (Zairian) proverb says it all: "The worm inside the beans destroys the seed with relative ease." Dependency is a systems problem. It is destroying the church from the inside. When I lived in a Spiritan formation house in Toronto, Canada (1975-1979), everybody contributed to the financial running of the house. Students doing their first degree in the university were studying and also doing part-time work to earn their living. In this way they could participate in the discussion of the house budget with dignity. When I was on my way from Canada to Congo Brazzaville, in 1979, to join the staff (all French Spiritans) in the regional seminary, I spent two days in the Spiritan provincial house in Paris. The bill was sent to me a few weeks later in Brazzaville. In Nigeria such a passage will be recorded under hospitality, especially in the case of one who is going to cooperate with a project of the province. In France it is important to state clearly who takes responsibility for costs. One cannot take anything for granted.

But generally in Africa we are continuing a system of irresponsible formation. Some even exaggerate this by thinking that simple gardening and manual labor take too much time from the students. We cultivate a bourgeois and irresponsible clerical class totally removed from the realities of life on the continent and also removed from the realities of adult life. Jeanne Diop-Yansunnu recommended to the African Synod that "all formation houses for priests be integrated within the local community instead of being large impersonal institutions." In this way priests will be "in touch with reality." In order for them to learn how to be "servants of society and not simply teachers or leaders," unity with laypeople is of the utmost importance.[29] Mrs. Yansunnu's call agrees with the viewpoint of Cardinal Thiandoum that the priest should be "in solidarity with the real living conditions of the people at large." However, in order to do this, the priest must have already learned to live in and to overcome those conditions.

The emphasis on formation of priests and religious during the African Synod was necessarily directed towards diversification, closeness to the living conditions of the people, and expertise. Formation of the priest as a person "of cult" is important provided that his involvement in the world is fully recognized as worship (cf. Rom 12:1-2). The African "priest" and "Levite" "preoccupied about worship and culture," according to Archbishop Zoa, intervening in the 1994 synod, should be given the opportunity "to get close to the man," "to see him, not to be distant, to have pity, to approach, to bind up wounds by pouring in oil and wine, to take him and put him on his mount of hope, to lead him to the inn and to take care of him (cf Lk 10:31-37)."[30]

It is not sufficient to live with the people or to locate the formation houses in their milieu. In addition, those pursuing priestly and religious vocations must be creatively educated to lead. To escape from being simply submerged in a situation of dependency, trainees should be taught to acquire the habit of critical reflection. This will endow them with the power to reflect and to act coherently in the situation of dependency in order to change it. In this way they emerge as free persons: enjoying the creative freedom of the children of God, they become competent to serve in freedom and to lead others into freedom.[31]

The emphasis on diversification and education for leadership, for priests and religious, has the ultimate aim of creating in them the potential to fully participate in dialogue with the temporal order, where the laity, also full members of the church, fulfill their ministry. The political and economic domains, issues of finance and material welfare for women and men in this world, are not evil. A certain dualistic

attitude in our clericalized church has made participation in these domains, if not totally soiled, at least unworthy of the good Christian.
But these affairs, according to Vatican II, must be illumined by the
gospel, renewed and organized by the laity in accordance with the
mind of Christ and to the praise of the Creator.[32] The leadership role of
the priest is necessary to reestablish in the church a holistic approach
to ministry which sees the involvement of laypeople in the economic
and political domains as an invaluable manifestation of the life of the
church.

With the collapse of education in Africa and the lack of credible
leadership for the youths in cities and rural areas, the churches, which
pioneered education during the colonial period, will make their presence felt in the reconstruction of Africa through participating in re-
educating the youth to make Africa self-reliant. Leaders in the church,
religious and priests, should not only be obliged to consume less but
also see their vocation of serving the Kingdom as fulfilled in investing
all energy in the reeducation of the African youth. If seminary formation lays less emphasis on subservience and stresses self-confidence,
hard work, self-reliance, self-sacrifice, and uprightness, along with an
intensive spirit of collaboration, the church may provide servants and
leaders who will participate with courage and dignity in the reconstruction of Africa.

Hesitant efforts are being made to restructure seminary formation
or to emphasize greater integration with the milieu and to expose candidates to greater appreciation of self-reliance. In the Spiritan theologate
in Enugu, practical agriculture has become an obligatory course for
the years in theology. This is only symbolic; and there are some who
wonder what relationship such a practical course has with seminary
formation! Many seminaries devise ways of maximizing internal con-
tributions to their budgets beyond the subsidies necessary for all educational institutions; and they are also teaching the young people to
face the real conditions of life in Africa. The need for a change has
been faced in a stronger way in an experimental program in Madagascar. In a pilot project for this renewal of priestly formation, "candidates live in simple houses in the midst of the people and share their
poor conditions." They cultivate their own rice fields and look after
their houses and environment as a way of contributing to their maintenance. During this formation period, which lasts longer than the traditional, candidates are in tune with the realities of Madagascar. Ac-

cording to Archbishop Albert Tsiahoana of Antsiranana, these realities form the basis of theological reflection which links the gospel to the life experiences of Madagascar and interprets life in the light of the gospel.[33]

The general feeling in our church in Africa is that neither the seminarians, nor the formators, nor the priests and bishops, nor the laity are happy with our present condition of dependency. No able-bodied, intelligent, committed, and disciplined person with a vocation to serve the church of God in the African context will feel at ease in such a situation. But this unhappiness has not been clearly articulated, nor has there been a clear alternative apart from recurring calls inside and outside Africa to simplify the lifestyle of the clergy. These calls are far from being heeded. In Nigeria, the way money and wealth are employed as principal indicators of success among priests has reached a level of scandal. The popularity of healing ministries and the multiplicity of rituals which play on the superstition of the people (whether rich or poor, illiterate or literate) are not unconnected with the financial viability of such projects. In addition, priests in contact with foreign agencies create a warped image of life in Nigeria to attract the sympathy and financial assistance of Europeans.

The church in Africa needs a major shift away from dependency. There must be a major shift in the way the church is conceived and ministry in the church is understood. The dependency syndrome is only a consequence of the seigniorial definition of, or at least the practice of ministry in, the church. Our bishops see this dependency as an anomaly. But they do not see its connection with our understanding of ministry. We should look at the root causes instead of the symptoms of our malady.

The church in Africa needs to completely accept Vatican II and carry it forward. This means going through a process of renewal which immerses us in the sources of the Christian tradition (especially the Christian scriptures and the Fathers) and facilitates our witness to the Kingdom in the prevailing sociocultural conditions of Africa. The major shift to reconstruct the church in order to make it bear witness credibly to the Kingdom on the continent must be done in deep collaboration and not in splendid isolation. Dioceses, national and regional conferences, and SECAM must work together in this gigantic move to restructure the church in Africa. Distances, poor communications, language barriers, and poverty may have rendered cooperation at the continental level very difficult (Thiandoum's opening report, no. 6). But I should like to suggest strongly that the lack of political will (Nkrumah) is responsible for the endemic problems in the structures and running of SECAM. If there is the political will to be fully church and not simply to be dependent on the Roman patriarchate, there is no reason why communication should be so difficult on the regional African and continental levels. There is no reason why church leaders should respond more quickly to Rome than to the duty of making SECAM a stronger force for the unity of Christian witness on the continent. It is when we have realized the importance of this shift in the notion of being church and in our style of ministry that the problems of self-reliance and self-sufficiency will be thought out and resolved in the formation of our youth.

CHAPTER 6

Service in the African Church:
An Alternative Pattern of Building Society in Africa

The church exists to proclaim and bear witness to the Reign of God. As the new Israel of God, she realizes already in her assembly what she proclaims by word and deed as an alternative way of living relationship. The style of ministry in the church is, in my view, the most eloquent testimony of the emergence of an alternative society in face of the dictatorships and the spirit of competition and domination which characterize governance and business in Africa and the world.

The 1994 Synod of Bishops for Africa gave a clear signal that the church in Africa wishes to chart a new course for relational leadership. No doubt the synod Fathers were aware that the present style of being church in Africa, as elsewhere in the world under the Western patriarchate, not only is dominated by the clergy but is clericalized. Consequently, it is interesting how the interventions in the general assembly of the synod, according to available statistics, show that issues related to the laity and Small Christian Communities (SCCs) loomed large as new structural elements for the emergent African ecclesiology. For example, while issues about priests and religious came up nine times each during the interventions, the laity and SCCs came up thirty and twenty-seven times respectively. Of course this does not mean that the laity are emerging as more important than the clergy or religious in a new understanding of evangelization in the year 2000. Instead of a major shift in direction, I see a major shift in concern. But this major shift in the concern of the church will ultimately influence a new direction in restructuring the church

104

to make her witness more convincing in the modern world.

What the interventions in the synod appear to indicate is the desire for a new kind of clergy, a new kind of ministry. The Fathers want "future priests" who will be true servants and animators of the Christian community. They want people who will be formed to work with and to recognize the laity as full members of the church. As one synod Father said, "They [the laity] are the church and their mission is the mission of the church." The laity do not simply want to observe what the clergy are doing; rather, they want to participate and make their contribution to the upbuilding of the church-community. It is because of a poor theology of baptism and a clericalized ministry that the laity have been denied their dignity in the church. Consequently, the wish was expressed to reexamine the whole area of "shared ministry" and to apply the principle of "collaborative ministry" as an essential ingredient of the African church.[1]

This shift in concern prompted the emphasis on the SCCs. Already, in the synod of 1974 and the Fourth Plenary Assembly of SECAM in 1975, the SCCs were adopted as the ideal pattern of evangelization in Africa. The SCCs are the cradle for the flowering of the new pattern of "collaborative ministry" foreseen by the African Synod. In the SCCs the people of God (the laity) learn to assume their responsibility in the church. No wonder that in the final propositions submitted to the pope, the synod Fathers advised that the family and the SCCs should be consulted for the choice of candidates for priestly ordination (no. 18).

If inculturation emerged as the dominant theme of the African Synod, relational ecclesiology, or the ecclesiology of the church-family-of-God, also emerged as a happy metaphor for the realization of the propositions of the synod. The Fathers invited theologians to explore African ecclesiology from this perspective (proposition no. 8). Sanon summarized the basic experiences of this ecclesiology in the field as follows:

We live the tradition of the Church communion, the Church family, the Church fraternity under the form of:
—basic ecclesial communities;
—living ecclesial community;
—basic Christian community;
—basic family community.[2]

Sharing Life and Gifts in the Church-Family

What emerges from the analysis of the organization of African societies made earlier in this study is that the community or society looms large. Its emergence is tied to ancestral history or memory. Consequently, the world of spirits is very much part of the human world and is a vital dimension for the humanization of the world. A similar situation is noted in the emergence of the church, which is the sphere of the operation of the Spirit of Jesus, the Spirit of God.

It is true that membership in the church is through the conversion of individuals. But, as the new Israel of God, or the People of God, the church is neither conceived nor experienced as a collection of individuals. The narrative of the church's emergence is clothed in myth— the sacred recital embedded in ancestral memory. It is rooted in the recital of the experience of the death and resurrection of Jesus. Neither in the African tradition nor in the story of the origins of Christianity do we see a conflict between the individual person and the constituted community. The modern Western experience of individualism, which sometimes sees the society as a threat to the interests of the individual and which may define society as a collection of individuals, is alien to these early community traditions. Instead of the community swallowing up the individual, the gifts of individuals are brought together to create humane community living that satisfies the aspirations of each and all.

Recent studies of distress in urban and rural Africa (for example, in Zaire and Cameroon) point to the frequent recourse to witchcraft as a way of taking revenge against some members of the society. Jealousy against wealthy members of society finds expression in sortilege. I am inclined to think that such an "imaginary" recourse to the metaphor of witchcraft in order to interpret social inequalities is indeed ingenious. Witchcraft functions as a metaphor for balancing relationships in societies in which the relational notion of person, as displayed in community, dominates. This relational notion is being threatened by the radical individualism of the modern world. Africans appreciate wealth. But wealth accumulated must always be at the service of the community. The jealousy which finds its expression through witchcraft is, in the final analysis, the expression of anger at the individualistic hoarding of goods, goods that should be utilized creatively for the common welfare. Thus, positively, witchcraft points to a value in danger of disappearing. It is a symbolic way of rejecting the hollow personality and empty patterns of relationship characteristic of utilitarian and expressive individualism. The project of a new ecclesiology of the church-family may help the African church to bear witness to the preservation of relational depth in the interaction of humans in the modern world.

Spirit Ecclesiology as Relational Ecclesiology

The dominant aspect of the dimension of spirit, as revealed in the sacred recital of the creation of each individual person in African societies, finds echoes in the creative manifestation of the Spirit of Christ in the emergence of the church-community.

In West African societies, as I pointed out above, the composition of the human person is expressed in a multiplicity of relationships. The spiritual element of the person is one of the fundamental dimensions expressed through the metaphor of relationship. This spiritual element is connected with God and is the creative genius which embodies the destiny of the human person. The Igbo call this spiritual dimension *chi*. Among the Asante it is called *okra*, while the Yoruba and ancient Egyptians call it *ori* and *ka* respectively. It is a way of stating clearly, in mythic language, that each person is a unique creation, a unique concern of divinity, an intimate of God the creator. As Achebe put it:

> The idea of individualism is sometimes traced to the Christian principle that God created all men and consequently every one of them is presumed worthy in His sight. The Igbo do better than that. They postulate the concept of every man as both a unique creation and the work of a unique creator (*Chi*) which is as far as individualism and uniqueness can possibly go.[3]

Among the Igbo this spiritual element is the basis of the creativity of the individual person in community. Success or failure, good luck or bad luck, which is assessed always in relational terms in the community, is expressed in this symbolic metaphor of the spiritual dimension of the self.

In the Christian dispensation, the presence of the Spirit of Jesus or the Spirit of God in the church-community generates intimacy with

God and creates the favorable conditions for creativity: the creative liberty of the children of God. As I pointed out earlier, those born (baptized) into the church-family are made children of God through the indwelling of the Holy Spirit—a Spirit which prays within each one of them (Rom 5:5; 8:9, 14-16). It is this indwelling Spirit which bestows gifts on each member of the new family of God for the upbuilding of this same family (1 Cor 12; Rom 12:4-8). This personal and individual link with the Spirit in the church-community is the basis of the freedom or liberation of each Christian. It is the freedom to create a better community, a renewed African community, a better world.

In the church-family where caring, solidarity, acceptance, dialogue, and trust[4] are characteristics of the warm relationship in the Spirit, the newly born Christian is fundamentally liberated to live an integrated, related, wholesome, holy life. This image of the church-family, which is fundamental to the call for a renewed African ecclesiology, demonstrates that inculturation is very far from watering down the Christian experience. The Synod of Bishops for Africa was quick to dismiss such fears. Cardinal Thiandoum summed up the feelings of the synod Fathers in his report after the interventions.

> It can be said that inculturation emerged as an overriding concern at this Synod. It concerns every aspect of the life of the Christian in Africa; it is the marriage of professed faith and concrete life. Inculturation has nothing to do with seeking a cheap and easy Christianity, rather its final aim is sanctity in an African manner.[5]

Inculturated ecclesiology draws both the church-community and individual Christians into greater intimacy with the Lord-Spirit. African ecclesiology moves each believer to a dynamic relationship with the Lord and with the community of faith.

Charisms and Creativity

The presence of the Spirit which fills the community and which dwells in each baptized Christian becomes manifest through the diverse gifts bestowed by the Spirit for the upbuilding of the community. Each baptized Christian is endowed with the gift of the Spirit as the Spirit wills. Each charism is a way of giving internal coherence to each Christian. It is a way of liberating each Christian from being closed within the self, so that he or she may be fully involved in the service of the community. As the church does not exist for herself but for the Kingdom, the gifts of the Spirit given to each Christian are for the purpose of propagating the same Kingdom (cf. 1 Cor 12:4-11). New Testament authors often fall back on rich Old Testament metaphors to describe the presence of the Spirit of God in the midst of the baptized as transforming the body of Christians into "a chosen race, a royal priesthood, a holy nation, God's own people" (1 Pt 2:9), "a kingdom and priests serving our God" (Rev 5:10; 1:6). This corporate sanctity of the kingly-priestly people, which makes them the competent servants of God or the propagators of the Kingdom, is well developed by the ecclesiology of Vatican II.[6] It is a sanctity which is best understood when expressed in the warm language of relational ecclesiology. Each Christian enjoys intimacy with God and at the same time lives a life of warmth, solidarity, and intimacy within the church-family, and, consequently, ministers in solidarity to the community and the world in order to transform the world. Our church-family is a church not only of the "head" but essentially of the "heart."

Often times those of us in the historical or missionary churches wonder why the sects and the independent churches (called African Christianities by some) have such success. Compared with the missionary churches, they arouse more participation and engender more fulfillment among their members despite the fact that the formation of their church leadership is in many ways rudimentary. We must appreciate the fact that many of these churches tune into the dimension of spirit, which is vital to the African notion of person. The "in" of the Spirit of God, who makes his home in the community and in each individual Christian, is also the "opening out" of the spirit of the community and of individuals to creativity. I have described elsewhere this impact of the Spirit in the community in terms of liturgical gestures. The gesture of folding the hands and placing them on one's breast, prevalent in the church since the twelfth century, not only indicates personal and interior prayer. It also expresses the individual and private orientation of religious practice as opposed to the communal opening out of the *orans* pattern (arms outstretched). The *orans* pattern represents a different kind of liturgical spirituality—"opening out," "leaving one's flanks open," "getting hurt," "warmth of love," and so on.[7] This spirituality of "opening out" is best realized when full value is given to the dimension of spirit within the church-community.

While the missionary churches (especially the Roman Catholic church) hold such charisms suspect, the independent churches delight in and even exaggerate such manifestations of the Spirit. The creativity which is embodied in the charisms both builds the community and heals the individual Christian. Aside from their exaggerations, the charisms experienced in the independent or "spiritualist" churches are in tune with the African universe and with the early experience of the Christian church-community. The services that the Spirit of God causes to be rendered to the community and the world are multiple, and they are communicated through these gifts. Christians become wholesome persons by the act of rendering this service.

Spirit-Presence and Wholeness

One must emphasize that the grace of the Spirit, and the services which go along with it, liberates both the community and the individual Christian, moving them towards integral living. Often times the African tradition interprets certain illnesses as signs of the special presence of, or invasion by, a particular spirit. The person is healed by undergoing a whole ritual process. The discernment of which spirit is active around him or her enables the community and the individual to identify the charism and keep it under control. In this way the process of determining what services the spirit is inviting the person to fulfill for the good of the community causes healing to be effected. Healing and equilibrium are not understood as inactivity (entropy). Healing is rather the recovery of one's whole self for creativity within the community. Thus the healing of the individual person is also the healing of the community.

The multiplicity of healing homes among independent church groups and the popularity of the healing ministry in the mainline missionary churches should come as a surprise to no one. However, the unfortunate incidence of the so-called "priest-healers" in Nigerian dioceses who remove themselves from the community arises from the failure to understand that both the community and the individual are healed in the legitimate and orderly exercise of charisms within the community.

What we should learn from this is that the Christian community should show concern for the integral welfare of each and every Christian. This is a crucial point for the liberation and health of the community itself. If Christians feel fully at home and cared for within their communities, their gifts will be fully deployed for the witness to the Kingdom. I already mentioned above the *agape* that rules relationships in the community and among communities. This *agape* is not limited to collecting money for needy Christians and communities. It concerns the total human and spiritual welfare of communities and individuals. As Paul put it in his apology: "And, besides other things, I am under daily pressure because of my anxiety for all the churches. Who is weak, and I am not weak? Who is made to stumble, and I am not indignant?" (2 Cor 11:28-29). African traditional communities, and the independent churches who learned from them, make such concern a priority. The ecclesiology of the church as a family or the church as a fraternity builds on this same concern. This is what Paul sums up in his letter to the Thessalonians as *philadelphia* (love of the brothers and sisters, 1 Thess 4:9-10).

The Indwelling of the Spirit and Full Human Rights

The love and care within the church-family, which is the source from which communities and individuals draw the energy to witness to the Kingdom, make the church the principal place for the recognition and defense of the rights of individuals. The recognition by the community of the gifts of individuals and of the needs of these same individuals bears the principal testimony that the community is the field of the operation of the Spirit of God. More than secular institutions, the Christian church has reason to defend the rights and dignity of each human person and each community. Any action that reduces a community or an individual to a subhuman level has more reason to be resisted within the church than in secular institutions. Any discrimination based on race, age, sex, or social standing has more reason to be rejected within the church-community than in secular institutions. For all humans are created in God's image, all Christians are children of God, and the indwelling of the Spirit of God is enjoyed by each and all. Just as the community is the subject of rights, each Christian (indeed each human) is a subject of rights. Unfortunately, from the time the Christian church and the secular dictatorships entered into an unholy alliance, rights of individuals and communities became infringed upon as a matter of course.

In the Christian church, a renewed African ecclesiology of the church-family should learn from African communal living that each community and each person can enjoy an integral, wholesome, holy life through the recognition of the indwelling Spirit in both the individual and the community. This recognition makes available to the Christian family and to the wider world services arising from those gifts bestowed by the Spirit of God. The call by the synod Fathers for "collaborative ministry" and for the creation of "lay ministries" in the SCCs is a step in the direction of recognizing the plurality of gifts and the many colors within the local church-community.

The recognition of the gifts of communities and individuals, of the rights of communities and individuals, is basic to the understanding of ministry in the church. It shows that fundamentally all members of God's family are graced (filled with God's particular gifts). All communities have their particular gifts which they bring to the communion of churches. No member of the church-family has an origin different from other members, though each has his or her own particular gifts. There is no question of any member being superior to any other member. In other words, no one, apart from the Son of God, the Head and Master of the church, is more a child of the common Father of all in the one church which is the Mother of all. All are begotten through the same ritual process of baptism in "water and Spirit." Ministries and services are exercised for the well-being of the community; through them the church-community bears witness to the Reign of God in the world. As Mgr. G. Philips put it, "Some were established as teachers by Christ, stewards (dispensers) of the means of salvation, and pastors, not over the others but for the benefit of the others, not *super alios* but *pro aliis*."[8]

Small Christian Communities: A Cradle for Rethinking Ministry in the African Church

The strong feeling during the African Synod that the model of Small Christian Communities offers the best pattern for the renewal of ecclesiology in the African church needs to be addressed seriously.

The SCCs go by various names. According to Sanon, the various versions of SCCs in Africa are called "basic ecclesial communities," "living ecclesial community," "basic Christian community," or "basic family community." They are all ways of living the tradition of the "church communion, the church family, the church fraternity."[9] The experience is very strong in Eastern Africa, in Zaire, and in some French-speaking West African countries such as Burkina Faso. During the African Synod the SCCs were projected as a viable model of renewing the church-family from the grassroots. That many bishops found it necessary to share their stories of the SCCs shows their faith in these experiences for the upbuilding of the church in Africa.

Opting for the SCCs

The bishops of the AMECEA region made a decision in 1973 to restructure their church and reorient pastoral activity according to the pattern of the SCCs.

> We are convinced that in these countries of Eastern Africa it is time for the Church to become really "local," that is: self-ministering, self-propagating and self-supporting. Our plan is aimed at building such local Churches for the coming years. We believe that in order to achieve this we have to insist on building Church life and work on the basic Christian Communities, in both rural and urban areas. Church life must be based on the communities in which everyday life and work takes place; those basic and manageable social groupings whose members can have real inter-personal relationship and feel a sense of communal belonging, both in living and working. We believe that Christian communities at this level will be best suited to develop really intense vitality and to become effective witnesses in their natural environment.[10]

This option was not simply a passing idea. In another AMECEA meeting in 1976 the adoption of the pastoral plan and ecclesiology of SCCs was confirmed. Also SECAM during the 1974 synod and during its fourth general assembly in 1975 made a clear option for the SCCs. In their declaration during the 1974 synod the African bishops expressed their option for and outlined their program of the SCCs.

> The Bishops of Africa and Madagascar emphasize the essential and fundamental role of living Christian communities: priests, religious and laity united in mind and action with their Bishop. It

is the clear task of these communities rooted and integrated as they are in the life of their peoples, to search deeper into the Gospel, to set the priorities of pastoral planning and activity, to take the initiative called for by the mission of the Church, to discern, in a spirit of faith where there can be continuity between culture and Christian life and where cleavage is necessary in all aspects of life that hinder the penetration of the Gospel.[11]

The resolutions of the 1975 SECAM plenary assembly endorsed the decisions of the previous year.

SECAM points out strongly that the Church of Christ is a communion and that this aspect of her life, which is the visible sign of the charity which animates her members, must be shown at all levels of the great ecclesial family. SECAM desires that particular attention be given to what are known today as "small communities," where each Christian, finding himself in a milieu suited to him, can live out his faith responsibly. One can note the following among the advantages of these small communities; fraternal communion is easier to achieve and live; they open the way for the incarnation of the Gospel message even in the simplest cultural background; this, however, requires, whether they be spontaneous or contrived, that they:
—Remain open to all other communities in ecclesial communion;
—Be founded on the Word of God;
—Be based on the Eucharist.[12]

The AMECEA Experience

In the AMECEA countries where this program has been most clearly articulated, not all the dioceses undertook the project of the SCCs. And not all the dioceses had a mapped-out action program. The more than ten thousand SCCs established in various dioceses in Eastern Africa do not all have the same experience. But studies have shown that in those dioceses where this way of being church has passed from discourse to action, an alternative community is emerging. To illustrate the Eastern African experience, I shall draw two striking examples from the contribution of J. G. Healey, an expert on SCC studies.[13]

In Same diocese, northeastern Tanzania, Bishop Lebulu and his pastoral coworkers adopted an action plan to restructure the diocese in line with a communion of communities ecclesiology. The SCC became the basic pastoral unit linked in communion to centers, and the centers became linked in communion to the diocese. No SCC unit is inferior to another, and so the idea of parish and outstation was eliminated. According to Healey, the diocesan synod of 1988-1991 examined SCCs in operation at the grassroots. "The starting point was the questions and felt needs of families and SCCs from the bottom up, not discussion from the top down. An important result was more autonomy and decision-making on the local center, level" (Healey, p. 68). Eight ministries are recognized in this new pastoral plan in Same diocese—catechetics, liturgy, vocations, development, counselling, stewardship, women, and youth. In this way the Same church is developing patterns suitable to what it sees as its true needs, and with resources within the reach of the community. It is not surprising that at the 1994 Synod for Africa, Bishop Lebulu called for the involvement of the body of the faithful (clergy, religious, and laity) in postsynodal "particular councils" on the episcopal-conference and provincial levels in order to adopt a common stand and strategy for the implementation of the resolutions of the synod. He also made a strong point for diocesan synods

> in order to reach the Church at its kernel—the hearts and minds of people, the family units and the Small Christian Communities in their social-economic, political environments and allow the People of God at the grass roots to evaluate, plan and follow-up the pastoral and development action and experience of the Church in Africa.[14]

In the diocese of Rulenge in western Tanzania, Bishop Mwoleka has been involved in developing the SCCs as a means for Christian transformation. In a seminal paper delivered in Rome during the fourth plenary session of SECAM (1975) he outlined the pastoral plan and theology which make the SCCs an imperative for Africa. His understanding of the Christian community is linked to the Trinitarian community and the paschal mystery—two realities adopted by the 1994 African Synod in describing inculturation and the SCCs. For Bishop Mwoleka, "Christianity consists in many persons sharing the one and the same life." What distinguishes Christianity from the other religions, according to him, should not be "truths" and "ideas" believed in but rather "to die and to come to life again in the hearts of those you love so as to share one and the same life with them. . . . For Christian life is not worthy to be called a life unless *it is shared*." This sharing is displayed in the SCCs. From the experience of the bishop of Rulenge, the SCC should not be confused with the parish structure, which is too loose and too large to be called a community. For people to effectively know one another and meet regularly, there should not be more than twelve families, who are real neighbors to one another, as members of a SCC.[15]

However, the diocese of Rulenge has moved beyond the SCCs. According to Bishop Mwoleka, "In most SCCs the exercise in living Christianity with and for others is neither constant [n]or intensive enough to meet the needs of our time." He instead launched a new pastoral initiative called the *integrated community,* which is a union of member families, single people, priests, and religious who bind themselves in a covenant with the single purpose of transforming the world. "No other concrete way of living in our time offers more promise for achieving the fullness of the Christian vocation than life in an evangelical lay community," says the bishop.[16] Members of this "lay community" make a total gift of their lives in a permanent commitment. Pastoral work such as catechetics and the animation of SCCs are not considered ministries superior to duties such as farming, taking charge of socioeconomic projects, cooking, and housecleaning. This ambitious program, of which the bishop is a full member, calls to mind the project of "Christian villages" which the early missionaries tried to build in order to establish physical boundaries between Christians and "pagans." But the laudable intent of the diocese of Rulenge is to create Christian community structures within society in order to transform society. However, like all such communities in Africa, they lack the financial self-reliance to fully determine their programs and the direction of their evangelical witness.

SCCs in the 1994 African Synod

The above examples from Eastern Africa form the background to the many interventions on the SCCs during the African Synod. There was a clear call for the adoption of the SCC model in the evangelization of Africa. In the words of Bishop Silota of Chimoio, Mozambique, to live the Christian message on the basis of "African communitarianism," "the SCCs seem to be the only way for the true evangelization and inculturation of the African Church." The SCCs put one in one's own milieu to confront the problems of life. If the SCCs are fully taken into consideration, a "new Church structure" would emerge, and there would be an "evangelization which would involve the whole person." Consequently, according to Bishop Silota, "we make a warm appeal to this Synod that it will once again declare the superior importance of the SCCs within the Church's evangelizing mission."[17]

One of the strongest remarks about SCCs came from Archbishop Mayala of Mwanza, Tanzania. For him, the SCCs are "the best way for us of being a Church in our African countries." He cried out against the obstacles posed to evangelization by the "ingrained institutional and hierarchical model of the church and the pre-Vatican II mentality," which were prejudicial to the full involvement of the faithful in proclamation. He even reproached the presynodal *Instrumentum Laboris* (no. 26) for its incorrect claim that other members of the church "share" in the "apostolic mission" of the bishops. Rather, he pointed out that, according to the teaching of Vatican II, there is a basic equality of all the faithful in the upbuilding of the Body of Christ; the one mission of Christ is shared by all Christians, anointed by the Lord, through many ministries (*Lumen Gentium*, no. 32; *Apostolicam Actuositatem*, nos. 2 and 3). He then called for an urgent conversion of heart so that the lay faithful may be fully involved in evangelization as proclamation:

Unless we undergo such a profound change of mind and heart in ourselves, it will not be possible for most of us to recognize, accept and affirm the rightful place of the laity as agents of proclamation and give them the necessary formation to exercise properly their ministries.[18]

Obstacles to SCCs

The conversion of heart is not going to be easy because it affects the whole notion of being church and the practice of ministry in the church. Max Weber's authoritative study on the sociology of religion has shown that the elite of any society (the aristocracy) is generally conservative (past-oriented) in religious practice. They seek from religion chiefly the psychological assurance of their legitimacy. They are thus not carriers of a rational religious ethic, the ingredients of religious revolution or reformation.[19] This is applicable to the church in Africa. In the first place, there is a clerical obstacle to the SCCs since their adoption in principle by SECAM in 1974 and 1975. Second, despite the support of the hierarchy for this new way of being church, its appeal is more pronounced among the poorer classes than among the middle class.

The recent study of SCCs by Healey shows that in both urban and rural areas SCCs have an appeal and have been established. But most SCCs are composed of the poor, though there are some lower-middle-class or middle-class people. However, while it is common to find SCCs of multiethnic groups, "SCCs that are composed of a mixture of people from different economic classes are not common."[20] One may call the SCCs the church of the poor, like the Basic Christian Communities of Latin America. Women are more numerous than men, there are more girls than boys. It is the grassroots church of the poor and weak of society. It was the same story in early Christianity. Christian apologists were drawn into a spirited defense of Christianity against the attacks of "pagan" critics who were quick to remark the preference of Christianity for the poor and the underdogs. But the fact that the SCC is a deliberate pastoral program calls for sober reflection on these distinctions. The elite are more at ease with privatized religion, while the poor and the weak are happier with a religion which extends to all sectors of their life. The declarations of SECAM and AMECEA must be confirmed by synods and provincial councils, and lived in parish and diocesan assemblies.

It is also symptomatic of a partial approach to religious practice in the SCCs that group reflections rarely touch areas of social action but, rather, emphasize the caritative dimension. This may not only be explained by the cultural preferences of Africa but also by the type of Christianity which was received into Africa—a Christianity which did not connect action in the socioeconomic and political domains with the love of God and neighbor. Only a clear program of reform will be able to move SCCs beyond this inherited orientation.

But the fundamental conflict lies with the inherited parish structures and the various apostolates operating within these structures. Indeed, while some dioceses in Eastern Africa see the function of SCCs as replacing the parishes, others do not see the situation in that way. The resolution of SECAM in 1975 did not specify whether parish structures and sodalities are set aside by SCCs. It is unlikely that the bishops would see the SCCs in that light, since the experiences differ from country to country. A discussion group in the SECAM assembly of 1975 listed among the requirements of SCCs that "it should include all Christian neighbors without exception. It is therefore the smallest unit (next to the family) of the parish." And again, "It should be represented by one of its members at the meetings of the Lay Council on the Sub-Parish level."[21]

The evidence appears to indicate that pastors have not fully come to grips with reorganizing the structures of the church at the grassroots level with the model of the SCCs. The sodalities, which are very popular in Africa (unlike in the Latin American church), have difficulties getting along with SCCs. Some members of these sodalities ignore the SCCs or fear them as a threat. The popularity of the pre-SCC parish structure more often than not reduces the SCC to a prayer group instead of a new or burgeoning church structure for the renewal of the community and the transformation of society. Healey believes that about 10 percent of the established SCCs in Eastern Africa are close to the objectives of AMECEA in establishing the SCCs. And Magesa concludes, "The history of SCCs in the region, in two decades of the existence of the objective, is a story of failure of implementation of a beautiful and scriptural aspiration."[22] The appeal for SCCs of the 1994 African Synod may end up like former calls if effective action programs do not follow these declarations.

Monoepiscopal Autocracy and Clericalism: Chief Obstacles to the New Way of Being Church

Problems encountered by the SCCs in entrenching the localization of the church in its primary structure and in beginning the development of a new kind of ministry are fundamentally rooted in male clerical power. As I summarized elsewhere the evaluation of SCCs in 1986 in Eastern Africa:

Some dioceses have done little to encourage SCCs in practical terms. . . . SCCs are clerical-centred with little and at times no initiative from the laity. . . . Some priests fear that if such communities are not properly managed other sects may spring up. There has been over-supervision of the SCCs due to fears of the dangers of the emergence of "splinter groups" and "schisms." ... Thus SCC leaders are not allowed to take full responsibility. ... Other people do not like changes. They want to continue things as they always did. ... When the laity are responsible the clergy tend to be very strict. Good recommendations from the Christian communities are not welcome.[23]

Clericalism—An Incurable Disease

The problems of clericalism have not diminished with time, as the studies of Healey and Magesa show. Bishop Mwoleka, addressing the 1975 plenary assembly of SECAM, called our experience of clericalism an incurable disease.

> The root of the trouble is that we have a fixed idea of the church. At meetings like this everybody seems to agree that the church, of course, means all the faithful. But at the back of our minds and in our imagination, almost instinctively, the Church is always the Church of the clergy. The disease is incurable.[24]

The church in Africa inherited this pattern of clericalism from the missionaries, who, naturally, communicated the post-Tridentine image of the church. The training of the clergy did not permit any questioning of such structures. In fact, our bishops and priests have no evident interest in changing the status quo in this church, which is "essentially an *unequal* society" made up of those who "occupy a rank in the different degrees of the hierarchy and the multitude of the faithful."[25] The reason is that those who occupy rank and possess the authority for promoting and directing the church do not have a natural inclination to tell the multitude, who are led like a docile flock, that there is an alternative. The privileged clergy are the principal beneficiaries. However, they are also victims of circumstance because they are inserted within the highly centralized and autocratic world church (of the Western rite). In the graphic words of Maurier, the pyramidal command structure of the Roman Catholic church is an "imperial, monarchical, centralizing authority."

The structural changes introduced by the French revolution into the concept of power in the West did not affect the church. Rather, the church insulated herself and preferred an existence in splendid isolation as a feudal "perfect society." Consequently, in spite of the revolutionary changes instituted by Vatican II, the church still operates with structures that merit its study to be called "hierarchology" instead of "ecclesiology."[26] The situation is very well known: the bishop is the extension of the pope, the priests are extensions of the bishops, and the lay people are the commanded serfs in the feudalistic structure. Of course the theology of Vatican II rejects such a "hierachology." It, rather, prefers the theology of the People of God. But little has been done to put into practice this radical revolution of ecclesiology.

Overemphasis on Power

The consequences of this "power" ecclesiology are unhappy and in some cases disastrous for the life of the church. In AMECEA countries, according to Magesa, the picture is one of an absence of dialogue and a lack of respect of genuine rights. Documents arguing for a change are not lacking. In addition to the *Dogmatic Constitution on the Church* of Vatican II, Paul VI's *Ecclesiam Suam*, the 1971 Bishops' Synod on justice, and the resolutions on justice during the 1981 Sixth Plenary Assembly of SECAM in Yaoundé (Cameroon) are clear indications of the new way of being church and of practicing ministry in the church. However, instead of dialogue where interlocutors listen heart to heart and become friendly and available for the service of one another, we have a church of power, of rank and privilege, of "differentiation from" instead of "identification with." The situation which Magesa is describing does not prevail only in Eastern Africa. A Nigerian bishop addressing senior seminarians some years ago is reported to have underlined this difference in formulas such as "We are the church, you are not the church; the church speaks, you listen; we talk, you do the listening; we give directives, you obey; you are there, we are here; we send you, you go!" The language and practice are not different from the tyrannies which are called governments in Africa.

The situation is made worse when such an arrogant exercise of power is clothed with the aura of sacrality. I borrow from Leonardo Boff the characterization of this sacralization of power in the style of the Romano-feudal "sacred and cosmic hierarchy":

Its legitimacy comes not from below but from above, from the will of God. The higher someone is in this hierarchy the closer one is to God and so has a greater share in God's divine power. To obey one's superior is to obey God. . . . This style of authority is untouchable and not subject to any internal criticism. Criticism from within any of the orders is only possible from a higher authority. A questioning from below would be equal to a revolution in the universe. Thus, any thought of transformation is the same as an attack on God who is author of both the order and structure of sacred power.[27]

From the experience of sacred power in traditional African systems of social organization, this kind of autocracy is a caricature of life lived under the eyes of God and spirits, as I shall develop in my analysis below. It, rather, represents the pattern of absolute or autocratic monarchies in Arab-Moslem or Moslem-influenced kingdoms of Africa.

Dangers of the Abuse of Sacred Power—a Nigerian Example

The exploitation of "sacred power" to the benefit of the elite is indeed most unfortunate. In the Nigerian church, the negative effects are becoming more and more disquieting because of the so-called healing ministry by priests. The problem is reaching a point where there is a real risk of schisms or the emergence of sectarian groups led by "priest-healers." The root cause of the problem, as I see it, is intimately connected with the abuse of "sacred power" and the misunderstanding of order and charism in the church-community. This power operates in two ways. First, it is based on the naked denial of rights to laypeople in the church because they neither belong to the clergy nor are they religious. In the words of the saintly Pius X, their "one duty . . . is to allow themselves to be led, and, like a docile flock, to follow the Pastors."[28] All decisions are taken by the hierarchy at their various levels of operation—parish, diocese, and episcopal conference. The deep respect for the sacred, the awe and fear which accompany intercourse with the sacred and those in sacred ministry, inherited from the traditional religious culture, restrain the laypeople from resisting such exercise of power.

Second, there is a fascination with the gift or charism of healing.

Gifted priests and charismatics show little restraint in publicizing their "miracle rain" through "testimonies" in imitation of the fundamentalist (American-style) Christian groups.

The problem of "priest-healers" has not left the Nigerian bishops at ease. A conference or consultation held in 1991 in which most of the well-known "healers" participated does not seem to have introduced order and restraint in the exercise of this charism. Again I see the problem as related to the "sacred power" of the priest. In Port Harcourt, Onitsha, Enugu, Orlu, and Aba dioceses, to name a few, our bishops find it difficult at times to exercise their supervisory ministry over the powerful "priest-healers." The charismatic priests appear to be very conscious of their power—a power which is often times maintained through the exploitation of the superstitious and the irrational, of which distressed faithful are easy victims. The orderly exercise of charisms for the benefit of the community appears not to be uppermost in the minds of some "healers."

. The laypeople in Nigeria recognize and respect the authority of the bishops, but they are also awed by the sacred gifts of ordained "priest-healers." Some even wonder why the gift of healing is lacking in other priests! (Most so-called healers frequented by masses of the distressed in Nigeria are priests. I know of only one case of a laywoman who is so frequented. She performs rituals comparable to those of the "priest-healers.") The celebrated case of the interdiction of one of the famous "priest-healers" in Aba diocese because of his dubious ways of conducting the ministry led to the priest setting up his own association. A former professor of theology and commissioner in the civilian government, he has practically turned into a leader of a sect. Denied access to his former center, he now holds his assembly in a hotel auditorium. Others like him operate on the margins of the church. They attract clients. They will remain popular. Said one layperson, "He is an ordained priest! A priest of God is a priest of God whether he is interdicted or not!" Such sacrality of power around priests and healers resembles the impact of oracles among the Igbo. In a culture that does not tolerate autocracy, one leaves the final word to the oracles; the closer oracular declarations are to the popular feeling, the more popular such oracles become, and the more they are frequented.

Such a disquieting situation, as is the case in Nigeria, will keep on gathering momentum insofar as the image of clerical autocracy is maintained. We know that the Catholic church has set up, in principle, structures for dialogue and for more participation of laypeople in the church—from parish councils to diocesan synods to the grassroots SCCs. But actual practice is a different matter. Bishops, priests, and seminarians in formation know clearly who is absolutely in charge in the church. When, in addition to this power, which is not questioned, one possesses the charism of healing, one may need be a saint to be free from the intoxication of "spiritual power." More often than not, "priest-healers" become tin gods! Combining in their one person the power of seers, healers, and priests representing God, they receive the thank-offerings of grateful votaries. When challenged about their orthodoxy or orthopraxy, they claim either that "it works" or that "it is what our people want/need." And because they have been enriched through thank-offerings, they become untouchables, outlaws! One bishop, during the 1991 conference referred to above, confided to myself and a colleague, "We are afraid of them"! The fear that this use of sacred power may empower the "healers" to create their own sects is becoming a reality in Nigeria. A change in the theory and practice of ministry is called for in the Nigerian and African church.

From Clericalism to a Collegial or Collaborative Ministry

The issue is not whether "hierarchy" is fashionable or not. It is not a matter of whether we should democratize the church or not. The incarnational tension within the church implies that the church as an institution cannot ignore the structures of the society in which she is living. However, the fundamental issue for the renewal of the church is whether the Spirit of God is allowed full initiative in the assembly of Christians. It is a question of whether the church still remains the creation of the Spirit of the risen Lord to accomplish the mission confided to her by the Lord.[29]

Earlier in this study I emphasized the ecclesiology of Cyprian of Carthage and the clear ecclesiological and disciplinary options of the North African church. Cyprian's ecclesiology revolved around the oneness of the church and the oneness of the priesthood. The moral unity which pastors must always maintain is the symbol of the unity of the church realized in a local group that enjoys its autonomy but is linked in communion to other local churches. North African councils were held to resolve problems of the church of North Africa. The North African church showed herself competent to solve her own problems without being the less in communion with the Roman church. The oneness of the priesthood is symbolized in the primacy of the episcopacy of Peter. The Lord made him priest before the others, not to show any superiority, but to demonstrate the one priesthood. When some disciples decided to discontinue with Jesus (Jn 6:66-69), Peter replied for the church. This shows that the church is the people united around its pontiff, the flock united around its shepherd. He who is not with the bishop is not with the church.[30]

Cyprian's letter should be read within the context of the controversy over his election raging in Carthage. Felicissimus was the leader of the opposition. His views are also to be understood from the exalted image he reserves for the episcopacy, derived from his literalist reading of the Levitical priesthood into the Christian ministry: Christians should respect in the priesthood God's holiness, which is manifest in the priest. On the other hand, the holiness required of the priest is also derived from the Levitical law of purity.[31] However, despite the high sacerdotal inclination of Cyprian, the bishop of Carthage declared himself opposed to dictatorship in the exercise of episcopal power. In the thick of persecutions, his colleagues, the priests and deacons, wrote him to ask for his views about the *lapsi* (who fell away but wish to come back). They had to find out from him because one should do nothing without the bishop (*nihil sine episcopo*). The bishop of Carthage replied in Letter 14:4 in the following words:

Concerning the matter about which our brothers in the priesthood wrote me . . . I am unable to give an answer all alone. I made it a rule right from the beginning of my episcopacy, according to my personal opinion, to make no decision without your counsel and without the vote (suffrage) of the people.

Thus, just as it is important in the church to do nothing without the bishop, it is equally vital to do nothing without the presbyteral council, and to do nothing without the lay faithful. Indeed, for Cyprian, the vote or consultation of the people is fundamental in the election of the bishop. Despite the fact that probably the ultimate vote lay with the neighboring bishops, Cyprian laid heavy capital on the vote of the people. This vote of the people, and of the members of the clergy, is the clear way of discerning the revelation of divine providence for the avoidance of human error (*praesumptio humana*).[32]

Cyprian's position shows us that the church as a people assembled around the pontiff, the flock gathered around the shepherd, is a unity based on communion and responsibility. Consultation and deliberation are important at all levels for the realization of the church. The pattern of administration is collegial, or to use the language of the 1994 African Synod, it is "collaborative" ministry. As Ratzinger and Maïer argued, referring to the style of Cyprian:

> One is not a priest alone but in the presbyterium of a bishop. One is not a bishop alone but in the episcopal college, of which the bishop of Rome assures the unity. And finally, one is not a Christian alone but as a member of a concrete "ecclesia," united around a priest placed in charge of it.[33]

In North Africa the laity could in no way be considered an appendage to a clerical church. The story of the Abitinian martyrs is a telling example. The forty-eight martyrs were arrested in the house of Emeritus while they were celebrating the Eucharist. Their bishop and presbyters had fallen away—having handed over the holy books to avoid imprisonment and possible execution. The community, unable to continue life as a Christian community without the Eucharist, found a presbyter from elsewhere to preside for them. After their arrest they were thrown into detention. While in prison, they held a council and excommunicated(!) the members of the clergy who turned traitors.[34]

We must insist that for Africa, and indeed for the world church, ministry in the church *should* be practiced in a collegial style—involving all the segments of the community.

Charisms as Services

Ministry is for the benefit of members of the church and not just for the fascination of some. Priests in Nigeria who parade gifts to fascinate the laypeople or to make money are comparable to the *ofeke dibia* (foolish and ignorant medicine men) of the Igbo tradition. It is pertinent that those whom the tradition refers to as *ofeke dibia* or charlatans are those who make real money from traditional medicine. They constitute a danger to the community because they could practice sorcery or poisoning to make money.

All those services surrounding that reality which is generically referred to in African tradition as *ogwu* (Igbo) or *nkisi* (Bantu)—meaning medication, herbs, gestures, or actions capable of providing healing or bewitching/poisoning—are considered beneficial social services when positively rendered. They are services to the society by gifted people (*dibia* or *nganga*). They are never primarily considered as a source of wealth or of the provision of one's livelihood. Indeed, gifts of that nature are never paraded, nor are they exploited for financial gains. Our gifted priests and laypeople in Nigeria, and elsewhere in Africa, who find themselves in healing ministries should revisit the traditional spirituality of being endowed with gifts for the service of the community, in order to appreciate the deep meaning of charisms for the upbuilding of the community as was lived by early Christianity (cf. 1 Cor 12). This will sink in better when ministry is learned as essentially service and not as the ladder towards rank and privilege. It is time for us to revisit this style of ministry as service in the New Testament and the canons of sacred ministry in the traditional African society.

Ministry "with Large Ears," or Leadership of Communities in the Service of Listening

A Manja Paradigm

Among the Manja of the Central African Republic the totem for the chief is the rabbit because this unobtrusive animal has "large ears." As is common all over Africa, the chief is considered to be very close to God, to the ancestors, and to the protective spirits of the community. He does not replace the ancestors. But along with other elders, he makes them present (represents them) in his person and behavior. The Manja underline listening as the most dominant characteristic of the chief. His "large ears" bring him close to God, ancestors, and divinities and close to the conversations taking place in the community. He has the last word because he speaks after having assimilated and digested the Word in the community. He is the guardian of the dynamic, life-giving Word which creates and re-creates the community. "Word" means truthfulness, fairness, honesty, communication.

One may legitimately compare this custodianship of the Word, imaged in the "large ears" of the chief, with the Bambara (Malian) philosophy of the *immensity of the Word*. The Word embraces the whole of humanity. When uttered, it heals and provides humane living. Such a sacred Word is "too large" for the mouth. This Word is an almost personalized phenomenon. No speaker ever totally masters or appropriates it; rather it belongs to the human community. Each sacred speech (of the community leader or of the representative of the community) approximates this Word.[35]

For the chief to be fair, he must be a patient listener. And this listening takes plenty of time. This is what is generally referred to as African "palaver": the liberation of speech at all levels of community in order to come close to that Word which is too large for an individual mouth, the Word which saves and heals. African palaver should not be confused with interminable, time-consuming, endless, aimless, useless discussion! Evidently, Cartesian or Aristotelian logic may find the African pattern of communication difficult to comprehend. An example of the impatience of Western logic with African palaver is the recent negotiations which were held to bring together the different political elements in South Africa to agree on multiracial elections. Seven world-renowned experts in diplomacy, including the famed American negotiator Henry Kissinger, and the former British foreign secretary Lord Carrington, provided their services to Nkatha, the African National Congress, and the National Party. Kissinger and the other Western negotiators left South Africa as soon as it was evident that Nkatha was not ready to cooperate. However, a junior member of the Kissinger-Carrington team, Professor Washington Okumu of the University of Nairobi, decided to continue the talking. Finally, "God" released the "Word" of understanding; and four days after the departure of the Western team, the dangerous impasse was broken, and Nkatha registered and participated in the historic multiracial elections.[36]

The sharing of the Word in Africa and the levels and patterns of listening and communicating vary depending on whether the system of social organization prefers authority in many hands or centralized authority. Many missionaries and colonial officials, who labored under a superiority complex, found it difficult to appreciate the kind of free speech practiced in Africa, which allows the creative Word to generate humane living in the community. This is especially the case in their encounter with communities which prefer authority in many hands. The Yoruba-born ex-slave, Bishop Adjai Crowther, demonstrated this frustration in his assessment of Igbo political culture.

One great drawback in the country is the utter disregard of lawful authority. . . . It is not too much to say that the moral conduct of the Ibos generally is characterized by a something approaching lawlessness. The people as a rule are impatient of control. It is no tribal partiality which induces me to say that in this respect they form a striking contrast to the Yorubas, whose respect for lawfully constituted authority is often shown by a loyalty which may be equalled, but can never be surpassed by the most loyal of civilized nations.[37]

The Challenge of the "Listening Chief" to Society and Church

The liberation of the Word is the best antidote against autocracy. The experience of dictatorships and the control of the mass media by government, where speech no longer is a means of communication but a tool for propaganda and lying, are far removed from the experience of communication, fairness, and truthfulness, which is the aim of speech and palaver in traditional African communities. In the name of African culture, those who like to hold the Word captive make the claim that as chiefs they have the last word. Mobutu propagated the slogan "one father, one mother, one country, one chief." His aim was to seduce Zairians into believing that he was the best thing that ever happened to Zaire. Many African dictators normally suppress the free press in their attempt to hold the Word captive. They are charlatans and terrorists. Instead of being leaders, they are hirelings and robbers who are there to steal and destroy. Communication, fairness, and truthfulness elude them because they have failed the first test of leadership in Africa: listening to the conversations going on in the community. Furthermore, they have failed to live under the gaze of the ancestors and God, in order to qualify to draw from the pool of that creative and healing Word which is "too large" for the mouth of one individual but which is so crucial for upbuilding the community. They have very "short ears" instead of the leaders' "large ears." They are hard of hearing. Indeed they are deafened by the noise of their propaganda.

It must be repeated over and over again, in the political community as well as in the church, that the chief, as the Manja tell us, begins by listening; he speaks only after having recorded the discussions going on in the community, so that his speech releases the healing Word of which he is the principal custodian, a Word which makes the community stand erect.

African bishops and priests love the image of the priest as chief. The elements considered for the now approved Roman Missal for use in the dioceses of Zaire make this clear. The crucial question studied when that liturgy was being put together was how a traditional chief would preside over the Eucharist if he had a grasp of its essential meaning. This image of the chief is displayed in the popularity of the leopard symbol in both liturgical vestments and the development of related liturgies (such as the liturgy for the profession of religious women). The leopard is the chief of animals. Liturgies being developed in Kumasi (Ghana) and Diebougou (Burkina Faso) also draw freely from the functioning of the chief within the community. This, in itself, is a positive orientation. Inculturation is taking its cue from the culture of the community. But it also shows a very positive appreciation of the understanding of ministry in the church. Instead of relating ministry to the service of a particular local spirit, it is understood as leadership of a community, which includes ritual functions.

However, to tune in fully to the Manja image of leadership, we fall back on the resources of our African tradition to retrieve the dynamic personality of the chief or community leader: a person living under the gaze of God, ancestors, and spirits, a person living in attentive listening to the community in order to accomplish adequately the ministry of custodianship of that Word which belongs to the community, the Word which belongs to humanity. Such an image of the chief is certainly unnerving for any individual. The integrity or sanctity expected of the church leader with "large ears" may even be more demanding than the sanctity of the priesthood according to the teaching of Cyprian of Carthage, a sanctity which Cyprian derived from the Levitical law of purity.

We must take care to underline that the image of the chief or community leader which will influence a truly Christian and truly African ministry in our church is not the bastardization of the image of the chief by African dictators, nor the imported Roman and feudal autocracy which dominates the present ministerial practice of the Roman Catholic church. The typical hierarchy in Africa is a serving "sacred power" or a selfless leadership, which is the polar opposite of autocratic or despotic rulership.

Liberating Sacred Power, "Hierarchy," through Initiation

The order (*ordo* of Tertullian) in the church and its hierarchical structure are sometimes argued, in Catholic ecclesiology, to be of divine origin. It is, however, strange that the key term *hieros* is totally missing in the New Testament description of ministry (*diakonia*). Certainly ministry in the church is connected intimately with the emergence of the church. From the constitution of the Twelve, who symbolize the renewed offer of God to Israel through Jesus, it is clear that their ministry is fundamental in the emergence of the "new Israel of God," which is the church. Second, the apostolic ministry (as distinct from the function of the Twelve) is so crucial that each branch of the church must in one way or the other trace its origin to the apostles. That is why, according to Tertullian, they are called "apostolic churches." When the apostles were sent forth by Jesus to preach after his resurrection,

> they then . . . founded churches in every city, from which all the other churches, one after another, derived the tradition of the faith, and the seeds of doctrine, and are every day deriving them, that they may become churches. Indeed, it is on this account only that they will be able to deem themselves apostolic, as being the offspring of apostolic churches.[38]

Bishops collectively succeed to this apostolic ministry, which is most essential or indeed indispensable (*origo necessaria*, Cyprian) for the unity and unicity of the Catholic church. According to Cyprian, the mandate of the bishops as the legitimate replacement of the apostles comes from Jesus Christ himself. In the approbation of an elected bishop by neighboring bishops, the apostolicity (legal succession to a see and not necessarily Tertullian's succession to orthodoxy) and catholicity of the local church are displayed.[39]

Other ministries and services arose within the church according to the needs of the gospel and following the movement of the Holy Spirit. Consequently, one has, for example, the ministry of the seven chosen to oversee the relationship between Jewish and Gentile Christians (Acts 6), and those placed in charge of the churches as presbyter-bishops (Acts 14:23; Tit 1:5), and the numerous services in the church, whose list is not supposed to be exhaustive (1 Cor 12).

Therefore the church cannot be conceived nor can she live without ministries. The church as an organization has need of leaders. In the apostolic and postapostolic church the ministry of the presbyter-bishop and deacon were the best known and universalized (Jerusalem, Antioch, Corinth, the church of the Pastoral Epistles). The operation of the Spirit of God within the community for the choice or election of the minister and the minister's posting, especially within the context of the liturgical celebration, lend an aura of sacrality to the responsibility of the minister. The leaders who met in the Council of Jerusalem and took decisions for the whole church were conscious that they were fulfilling a sacred duty.

> The brothers, both the apostles and the elders, to the believers of Gentile origin in Antioch and Syria and Cilicia, greetings. . . . For it has seemed good to the Holy Spirit and to us to impose on you no further burden than these essentials . . . (Acts 15:23-28)

In this way one may legitimately interpret the function of leadership in the church as an exercise of sacred power, "hierarchy." It may be more correct to speak of sacred ministry. But if this is construed to mean the establishment of *ordo* in the form of the Roman *ordo senatorius*, entrenching rank and privilege in the church-community, such an understanding of ministry will be totally against the prescription of the Master:

> You know that among the Gentiles those whom they recognize as their rulers lord it over them, and their great ones are tyrants over them. But it is not so among you; but whoever wishes to become great among you must be your servant, and whoever wishes to be first among you must be slave of all. For the Son of Man came not to be served but to serve, and to give his life as a ransom for many (Mk 10:42-44).

Service Is the Norm

Whatever may have been the later developments of Christian ministry in imperial Rome, especially after the Edict of Milan (313), the prescription of the Master remains the norm. After the church was granted the right to exist in the Roman Empire, and especially when Christianity became the state religion under Theodosius (fifth century), the ensuing clerical privileges led to the clergy being counted among the senatorial class and distinguished from the *plebs*, the people. However, despite this historical development, the command of Jesus is the fundamental and overriding Christian norm for judging ministry in the church. The service or self-gift of Jesus unto death influenced definitively the Christian notion of ministry as service *(diakonia)*. John's Gospel describes it as the last testament or will of the departing founder of Christianity in the arresting story of the washing of the feet:

> Do you know what I have done to you? You call me Teacher and Lord—and you are right, for that is what I am. So if I, your Lord and Teacher, have washed your feet, you also ought to wash one another's feet. For I have set you an example, that you also should do as I have done to you. Very truly, I tell you, servants are not greater than their master, nor are messengers greater than the one who sent them (Jn 13:12-16).

This testament of the Lord to his church on the eve of his passion is as powerful as, and the reverse side of, the eucharistic rite. Both the service and the rite, the one never without the other, make present the service of Jesus in the Christian community and the witness of the church to the good news of salvation in the world.[40]

Indeed, Teresa Okure has drawn attention to the deeper meaning one should perceive from the style of leadership that Jesus exercised and enjoined on his followers. Jesus' preference for the life of service and the imagery of the "waiter at table" are meant to introduce a revolution in the way ministry is perceived in the church-community. In the Jewish culture, as well as among Africans, "cooking and serving food is seen as a woman's work, not a man's work." Consequently, Jesus' imagery of leadership "was not only brand new, it was fundamentally counter-cultural (both politically and religiously) and even offensive to the dignity of the man." But the deeper meaning that Okure wants us to see in Jesus' predilection for this imagery is the quality of "mothering" or "caring" which should dominate Christian ministry:

> If Jesus freely chose to associate himself with the food-serving ministry of women in the gospels, it is because his ministry, his

life-giving leadership ministry, has a fundamental, natural re-
semblance to the specificity that is woman's, seen as "mother of
all the living" (Gen. 3:20). Because ultimately "As a woman
feeds her child with her own blood and milk, so too Christ himself
continually feeds those whom he has begotten with his own
blood."[41]

Of course the historical Jesus was neither a woman nor a biological
mother. But African women, and especially African feminist theologians, emphasize the need to "present mothering as a positive strategy
for community life that is to be practiced by all women *and all men*."
This is brought out in an Akan proverb which says, "It is not only a
woman who gives birth, a man does also."[42]

This fundamental value of mothering (to be distinguished from
motherhood) or caring or loving is a gift of the self which the Lord
instills at the very heart of the community and of its leadership. It is
best displayed in the context of the Eucharist, where he nourishes or
feeds his flock.

Ministry as Being Transformed into Eucharist

Official Catholic theology of the priesthood and the prevailing liturgical practice of the Roman rite like to link the establishment of the
priesthood to the original gestures of the Lord Jesus on the eve of his
passion (on Holy Thursday). This connects the institution of the Eucharist, understood as sacrifice, with the priestly ministry. Bishops
(and presbyters) have been associated with the presidency at the eucharistic celebration, considered as a sacrifice at least from the second
and third centuries. (The *Didache* may be the last evidence of the presidency of prophets.)

Though one may correctly follow Schillebeeckx in saying that "there
are no biblical grounds anywhere for a sacral and mystical foundation
to the ministry in the eucharist,"[43] yet I think that Catholic theology is
correct in establishing a close link between the emergence of ministry
in the church—and the founding of the church herself—and that original and foundational narrative of the eucharistic gestures. It is a narrative of the self-gift of Jesus as food for his friends. It is a narrative
condensing and interpreting the more lengthy recital of the passion or
the ordeal Jesus passed through in order to become the redeemer of

the world. This ordeal or paschal mystery is a passage, an initiation. Into this ordeal the Lord initiates all his followers.

If "servants are not greater than their master" nor "messengers greater than the one who sent them" (Jn 13:16), then ministry is not the simple action of presiding over the Eucharist; nor does ordination simply mean being bestowed with the power of being the instrument for transforming the bread and wine into the body and blood of Christ. Rather, ministry is the challenge of being transformed into Eucharist. It is essentially displaying, in the midst of the brethren and in the world, the service of the Master unto death. This view tallies with the rabbinic understanding of the messenger, the one who is sent (*shaliach*, or *apostolos*)—the authorized or commissioned representative of the sender of the apostle.[44] But it involves an additional and fundamental dimension of witness (*martus*) which excludes the inviolability reserved to the Greek messenger or herald (*kerux*), and makes the witness vulnerable like the Master.

Ministers or leaders of community are in this way the commissioned representatives of Jesus Christ (1 Cor 12:28) and the commissioned representatives of the Spirit-filled community (2 Cor 8:23; Acts 13:2f). They are elders who are witnesses of his sufferings (1 Pt 5:1) through their own sufferings. "This favor only I beg of you," wrote Ignatius of Antioch to the Romans, "suffer me to be a libation poured out to God, while there is still an altar ready for me. . . . I am His wheat, ground fine by the lions' teeth to be made purest bread for Christ."[45]

Initiation into Ministry—the Model of Jesus

The letter to the Hebrews sees the self-offering, passage, or paschal mystery of Jesus in terms of being initiated to become the mediator between the world of spirits and the human world. Jesus was drawn from the human community; he is the Son who learned obedience through his suffering. Drawn from the human community, he was totally tuned into the reality of human suffering. During his ordeal, he "offered prayers and supplications, with loud cries and tears, to the one who was able to save him from death, and he was heard because of his reverent submission" (Heb 5:7). His sacrifice was accepted and perfected (declared agreeable) by God. Having been perfected, he becomes the perfecter of his brethren: "For by a single offering he has perfected for all time those who are sanctified" (Heb 10:14; cf 5:9; 7:11; 12:1-2).[46] In other words, having been fully initiated in obedience to his Father, he becomes our initiator.

We become Christians through a process of passage or initiation which imitates his death in order that we may rise up to a new kind of life (cf. Rom 6:1-3). We become, thereby, partners or participants in Christ (Heb 3:14) or a kingly priesthood (1 Pt 2:9-10; Rev 1:6; 5:10). That is why we "look to Jesus the pioneer and perfecter of our faith" (Heb 12:2). Consequently, the Christian group, as a body and as individuals, bears united witness to the service unto death of the Master. This is its fundamental ministry in the community and to the world. When the community is fully aware of the Master's path of humiliation and self-abasement (cf. Phil 2:6-8), it will be impossible for the church to move from the language of service to that of domination, from the language of being slaves of all to the language and practice of rank and privilege. Service as the overriding experience of living in the family of God has set aside all manner of domination based on patriarchy and on special knowledge or gifts.

> But you are not to be called rabbi, for you have one teacher, and you are all students. And call no one your father on earth, for you have one Father—the one in heaven. Nor are you to be called instructors, for you have one instructor, the Messiah. The greatest among you will be your servant. (Mt 23:8-11)

To avoid the betrayal of this gospel, which has the sole intention of changing the ways of the secular world, of creating the alternative society which is the beginning of the transformation of the world, we must reread the injunction of the Master in terms of the resources of Africa in its social organization. We shall not betray the gospel through believing that a certain incarnational pattern ("civilizational model") of social organization is unchangeable.

Leaders in the church (especially bishops, priests, and deacons) prolong the service of the Christ within the community and for the salvation of the world. They undergo an initiation similar to that undergone by the elders or chiefs of African communities, and they operate like the leaders or masters of initiation. Fully tuned to the world of the spiritual, where Jesus the Christ is seated making intercession for us, they are in intimate relationship with God; they are God's elect through the vote or the acclamation of the people (as is the Alafin of Oyo, and as is the practice within the church of Cyprian's North Africa). As people implanted into the ancestral tradition through initiation and through legitimate succession to the custodianship of the ancestral heritage, one may truly call our church leaders "elders" and "founders or builders of the village (or community)." Like the leaders or masters of initiation, who are selected by the community because of the depth of their experience and, indeed, in imitation of the Master, the Christ, the initiated-initiator, one could apply the imagery drawn from the Sini (the Bobo genealogical recital) to the leaders of our church. One may thus look upon them, in their quality as leaders of community prayer, as "intercessors like unto God," "chief intercessors for the community," or "intercessors for the youth" (whom they initiate into the service of the community). Again as symbols of the compassion and *agape* that is the law of relationship within the community, one may address the church leaders, in terms of the heightened spirituality of the Bobo leaders, as "chief and father of the slave," "friend of the community griot or storyteller," "friend of the poor," and so on.[47]

Listening—the Overriding Metaphor

However, the most arresting imagery of being fully initiated into this ministry or service in the church is the image of the "large ears." The characterization of the leadership of the bishop in his diocese or of the episcopal conference in a region as a ministry "with large ears" is a good symbol for leaders working for the unity of the community and for effective communion or communication between local churches. Because it implies consultation or deliberation at all levels of community, it becomes an imagery which testifies, according to Cyprian, that the will of God may triumph in the church-community over human presumption or error.

The community as a subject of right, as the sphere of the operation of the Spirit of Christ, is built on collegiality through the collaborative participation of its members. It is necessary to underline that the Yoruba (of the Oyo kingdom) declare that the Alafin is a "divine king." Nevertheless, twice a day, there is deliberation over his manner of ruling, or rather leading, the community by seven powerful chiefs who are members of his cabinet. And there are other levels of control, as I pointed out earlier. This shows that the community has faith in its God; but God is best encountered in the conversations going on in the community for the benefit of the entire community. It has trust in the spirituality of its leaders, but this trust is best expressed through the free participation of all in deciding the orientation of their community. This participation is more direct or republican in those communities where the exercise of authority is in many hands.

The Christian community is all the time listening to the voice of him who has conquered death, the chief Shepherd who gave his life for his flock. The elders of the community are "witness[es] of the sufferings of Christ" (1 Pt 5:1). And as true witnesses (martyrs), they "feed" or "tend" the flock, not lording it over them (cf. Jn 21:15-16; 1 Pt 5:1-4). A leadership which cultivates the ministry "with large ears" makes it easier for the churches to listen, to hear, and to do what the Spirit is saying to the churches (cf. Rev 2:29; 3:22). This is the way forward for the church in Africa and for the world church. On this basis the church may challenge dictatorships and their propaganda, which undercut communion or communication at the expense of humane living.

Listening—Hearing Women in the African Church

When the synod Fathers of the Special Assembly for Africa were talking about collaborative ministry, they had their eyes on all the laity without distinction. There was great sensitivity to highlight the role of women in introducing a certain quality into the new model of church as family.[48]

The "listening" model of the church may, however, open up the church in Africa, and the world church, to empower her to a life of witness beyond the present practice of ministry in the Roman church. When the community listens to the Lord of the gospel, it may hear the gospel message in all its novelty. As an Igbo saying goes, "Drop the ear on the ground and hear the cry of the tiny ant [*agbusi*]." The "cry of the ant," the countercultural, constitutes the core of the novelty of the Lord's behavior and command. It is an explosion of Jewish culture, the explosion of African cultures. It inaugurates the functioning of a sociocultural group in a Christian way. This novelty is captured in a pre-Pauline hymn which was probably used in the practice of Christian initiation:

There is no longer Jew or Greek,
there is no longer slave or free,
there is no longer male or female;
for all of you are one in Christ Jesus. (Gal 3:28)

The marginalization of women in African cultures and elsewhere in the world is an area where the proverbial evangelical double-edged sword may be introduced into the culture. On the eve of the twenty-first century, says the 1994 synod, "the culture which gave identity to our people is in serious crisis"; consequently, "there is a fundamental need . . . for prophets to arise and speak in the name of the God of hope for the creation of a new identity."[49]

In traditional and modern Africa, women have generally exercised effective power in a corporate manner. A celebrated example in Eastern Nigeria was the 1929 Aba riots, the "women's war," which effectively overturned or modified colonial policy with regard to taxation and the installation of warrant chiefs. However, on the issue of individual rights and privileges, Africa has had its share of the oppression of women. In modern times the oppression and subjugation of women may have increased with colonialism and the practice of mainline Christianity. The two systems privileged the menfolk in employment opportunities and leadership roles.

It is a well-known fact that the contribution of women in the struggle for independence in Africa and in the liberation of Southern Africa from racism is considerable. But this contribution has not been compensated adequately through commensurate political responsibility. As Ali Mazrui summed it up:

As *combatants*, African women were part of the crusade for the empowerment of the continent. As *diplomats*, African women later represented the sovereignty which they had helped Africa to acquire in world affairs. But as *power-brokers*, African women seem to have been on the whole part of the periphery rather than at the center of politics.[50]

The Christian church has favored a practice of leadership which is characterized by patriarchal dominance. This practice derives from the Hebrew Scriptures and continued through the Fathers to our own time.[51] A revealing study of SCCs by Anne Nasimiyu-Wasike projects the need to evangelize the role of women in the African church. Wasike's study of two parishes from Kisii and Eldoret dioceses of Kenya shows that members of SCCs are principally women. The average ratio of women to men is 80.6 percent to 19.4 percent. Paradoxically, leadership of the SCCs continues to be dominated by men even in cases where there is only one male member. Wasike reports a particular case where a former male chairperson opted out of the group because a woman was elected chairperson. His reasons were, "Women are disorganized, lazy, have no ideas, are not able to plan, are always late for meetings, and they lack professionalism and ambition."[52]

Through ages of socialization the majority of women accept the subsidiary and complementary roles reserved to them in African culture and the Christian church. Our proposal of the ministry "with large ears" or leadership in the service of listening, which recognizes the initiative of the Spirit of Jesus in the church and which pays close attention to the conversations at all levels of the People of God, may lead to stronger leadership roles for women within the African church, upset human/cultural forecasts, and rejuvenate the church-community. Though this study has not the controversial question of the ordination of women in view, my comments may go beyond lay ministries.

I am fascinated by the multiplicity of ministries in the church of the Fathers, especially in the Syriac church of *Testamentum Domini*.[53] The offices most frequently mentioned by *Testamentum Domini* are, in the following order, bishops, priests, deacons, confessors, widows, subdeacons, deaconesses, lectors. During the eucharistic celebration, according to chapter 19 of this document, ministers (meaning members of the hierarchy) flank the bishop: the priests on his left and right, the widows occupying the whole of the left flank behind the priests, and, standing on the right flank behind the priests one after the other, the deacons, the lectors, the subdeacons, and the deaconesses. According to Arranz, widows may have been quite numerous to have occupied the whole left flank of the sanctuary behind the priests.[54] The more interesting point which concerns our discussion here is the ordination of widows and their ministry. The widow is ordained (*metasrhonuto*, the same term used for the ordination of the bishop, the priest, and the deacon). The ordination is in the form of a prayer said by the bishop in a subdued tone audible only to the priests surrounding the bishop. Our document does not talk about imposition of hands.[55] The widow's ministry, aside from service at the altar, is the celebration of the Hours, especially the night and early morning praises. Part of her social function is visiting the sick every Sunday; she may take one or two deacons with her during the visitation.

In evoking the practice of *Testamentum Domini* I do not have the intention of conceiving ministry as crowding everybody into the sacristy or into the sanctuary. I simply want to draw attention to the practice of a church which developed in a Semitic milieu which is noted for looking down on women. The listening church model cannot continue indefinitely to exclude women from ministry if the ears of the church-community are attentive to the Spirit and to the conversations going on within the community.

The Ministry "with Large Ears" and the Communion of Churches

The image of the chief or community leader "with large ears" favored in this study highlights two salient points. First of all, authority is exercised fundamentally for the integral well-being of the community. Second, this style of exercising authority is capable of mobilizing the community for its integral development and the achievement of its aims and objectives. This perception of leadership has the potential for facilitating relationship not only within the local church but also on the supralocal (universal) level of the church.

When authority is exercised for the integral well-being of the community, then the spiritual and material welfare of women and men living in their concrete life situations is the principal preoccupation of the service of authority. Authority is not there for the cultivation, protection, or defense of ideas or beliefs. Christianity is not a system of ideas and beliefs. Rather, Christianity consists in many persons sharing one and the same life; it consists in dying and coming to life again in those one loves so as to share the one and the same life with them (Bishop Mwoleka).[56] Thus what should be most crucial in the determination of the objectives of leadership in the church is to facilitate the love and sharing, the care for one another, in the imitation of Christ, which is the aim of the church.

The ministry "with large ears" which is described in this study disposes the leader to listen fully in order to facilitate a nonthreatening but progressive upbuilding of the Christian community. This is the way to render justice to each and all, and the way to make the community achieve its purpose of bearing witness to the Kingdom, the transformation of the world. During a festival mass of a newly ordained priest in my home town (Nnewi, Anambra State), the chief of the town (Igwe Kenneth Orizu III) was in attendance. The prayer of the faithful (bidding prayers) was spontaneous. Two women prayed for Nigeria and for all those involved in government. I was thinking they were going to pray for the health and progress of the chief and other government officials. But their prayer picked up a recurring refrain, *"ka onye obula nweta ihe luu-lu ya"* (that each and all may receive what they are entitled to in the society). In other words, the rulers should render equitable and distributive justice to all members of the society. It is not a prayer against the health or progress of the rulers, but for the realization of the objective of society—the well-being of each and all. The aim and reward of leadership is this well-being of each and all. One may compare this popular pattern of praying for leaders of civil society with Solomon's prayer for wisdom. The leader is not there for himself or herself, but for the welfare of the community.

I shall now try to apply this pattern of pastoral leadership "with large ears" to the communion of churches on the supralocal level, to the relationship between the local churches of Africa and the Roman church.

Renewing the Center—the African Family Model

In his book, *African Theology in Its Social Context*, Bénézet Bujo used the mortuary rites of the Bahema of Zaire to illustrate a possible model for the redefinition of the relationship between the churches, especially the relationship between the churches in Africa and the primatial church of Rome. The rites of a departed father of the family display how the life received from ancestors passes over to the children (through the sons in a patrilineal society) and is continued. Grains of millet are put into the hands of the dead parent, and the sons feed from his hands. Thus the sons receive strength from their father. The eldest son, or whichever son is more experienced and judicious, is installed as heir. His hands are placed on a cow's udder by his father's brother, and he begins to milk the cow. A lot of symbolism is connected with this custodianship of the ancestral property. The eldest symbolizes both wisdom and being close to the ancestors. He will feed the flock as well as redistribute the ancestral property equitably among his brothers. This ensures the survival of the family and the continued interrelationship among the brothers, despite the necessary independence of each brother as an adult. This is the obligatory pattern of facilitating the progress and intensification of the life received as a gift from the ancestors. To lay claim all alone to the ancestral property or to keep it solely for oneself is abominable. It is a crime against life and its enhancement.

This ancestral model of ecclesiology will make the ministry of Peter similar to the service the eldest brother renders to the ancestral family. As the eldest brother, the successor of Peter is concerned with communicating and intensifying that life received from the proto-Ancestor, the Christ. The successor of Peter must also realize that the other brothers have received the same life force from the same source (the Christ). Consequently, his presidency is directed towards encouraging a harmonious family life, but not meddling unnecessarily in the affairs of the other adult members of the family.[57] These points developed in the work of Bujo advance a creative interpretation of the family model of the church adopted in principle by the 1994 African Synod. In addition, following the Manja metaphor of "large ears," the eldest or wisest brother is the one who has developed the greatest capacity for listening to the will of the ancestors and to the conversations going on in the human community. This is the onerous task which is to be borne by the center (Rome) when it is renewed by the African family (social) organizational model.

Leadership at the Center—the Difficult Art of Oversight

The exercise of authority, as caring and warmth in the church-family on the local level, mobilizes all the gifts of the members of the community for the upbuilding of the community. Since these gifts fundamentally manifest the operation of the Spirit of Jesus in the church, this exercise in mobilizing all endowed members becomes an art of oversight. It is the art of the discernment of gifts for the good of the community and for the transformation of the world. In a nonthreatening pattern of ministry, each member of the community feels at home and displays his or her gifts for the re-creation of the community and the world. This brings out the fact that the many ways in which the gifts of the Spirit are manifest for the upbuilding of the community are the many ways of showing the initiative of God, or the independence of the Spirit, within the particular or local church. It shows the necessary openness of the local church to universality (always under the direction of the Spirit) and the unity of the local church, which is not threatened but strengthened by diverse gifts.

The independence and initiative of the Spirit in the church operates in a more intensive way on the supralocal level. Consequently, the presidency over the "assembly of charity" (Ignatius of Antioch) will require extraordinarily "large ears." It may be easier in a monocultural district of the church to discern what the Spirit is saying to the churches. But in the present multicultural world context where Asians, Europeans, and Africans live the paschal mystery of Christ, the discernment of the unity established in difference (Irenaeus, Gregory the Great, John Paul II) becomes an art which needs to be frequently tested by the vote of the people to confirm the operation of divine providence in the service of leadership and to limit human error (Cyprian).

From our historical survey of the Roman centralization which was achieved not by persuasion (as in the Nri tradition), but by force (as in the colonial legacy), and from the relationship between the church in Africa and the primatial church of Rome in the past twenty years, one must confess that the image of a centralized state which the Roman Catholic church bears (Ratzinger) appears to hold little hope for a "listening church" model. I shall summarize again the arguments of African bishops for pastoral leadership "with large ears" in the delicate management of relations with the Western patriarchate. I limit my examples to the synod of 1974 (which was followed by the SECAM Plenary Assembly of 1975) and to the 1994 Synod for Africa.

In his report on the participation of African bishops in the 1974 synod, Archbishop Zoa of Yaoundé told the 1975 Fourth Plenary Assembly of SECAM that "all the leaders of the young churches wish to take the destiny of their own church into their own hands." Within the "communion of the church," "the young churches of Africa and Madagascar" demand more responsibility in their church. "In view of this mission and in this perspective, the episcopal conferences claim *the right to greater liberty.*" The areas of this claim to autonomy are chiefly liturgy and catechesis, marriage, the formation to the priesthood and religious life, and ordination to the priesthood of presidents of communities. There was also a call for the revision of the "law and legislation of the Church . . . for the service of man and [to] favor his meeting with Christ" and for the creation of authentic Christian communities and the revision of the manner of cooperation with missionaries.

The interventions of the bishops on this issue of greater autonomy are better reported in their own words: "Episcopal conferences, therefore, have to be given greater freedom, Africa will be all the more loyal to the Holy Father" (Mgr. Yago, Abidjan); one must "take African norms into account; ecclesiastical legislation has to leave a lot to the initiative of the leaders of local churches" (Mgr. Bakpesi, Togo); "We maintain the declarations previously pronounced by our delegation to the synod, relating to the ordination of married men and the 'ad tempus' priesthood; we shall always be loyal to the decisions of Rome" (Mgr. Bayala, Upper Volta); "The central organizations of Rome [are] to be more trustful of Episcopal Conferences as regards, for example, the Liturgy, priestly education and religious life" (Mgr. Rakotondravagatra, Madagascar). The intervention of Mgr. Maanicus (Central African Republic) in the name of the conferences of Chad, Central African Republic, and Congo is given considerable space in Mgr. Zoa's summary. In sum it requests that "respective Episcopal Conferences be allowed to decide what initiatives to take as to the spiritual good of those under their charge . . . and not be brought down to a rigid application of Canon Law" and "that the answers of the Holy See to pastoral questions brought up by Bishops' Conferences be given only after a close examination and a genuine discussion with those on the spot, those who are Bishops responsible to God and the Native Church."[58]

Bishop Sangu of Mbeya, Tanzania, who summarized the reactions of the bishops before the 1974 synod for the Africa group, summed up accurately the feelings of the bishops during the synod. He noted that there is little danger or desire to be independent of the Holy See; the Holy Father is highly valued and his authority respected. But this does not mean a refusal of legitimate autonomy:

> But the changing conditions, and especially the coming-of-age of the African Church require a re-thinking of the relations between the African Churches and the Holy See; between the African Churches and the Congregation for the Evangelization

of Peoples; between the Episcopal Conferences and the Roman Curia, so that Episcopal Conferences could handle local matters which do not prejudice the universal church; relations too between Episcopal Conferences and Papal Legates should be clearly redefined.[59]

This instinctive blending of the imperative communion and the necessary autonomy is deeply rooted in African ancestral memory. Leaders of African local churches feel deeply that they belong to a large or extended family; and they want to share fully in the construction of this church in the world and to bear witness to the Christ. But communities are best constructed on the basis of plural listening—to both the visible and the invisible inhabitants of the universe. Even if it takes time, it is always profitable to dialogue. The best manifestation of the creative and life-giving Word is in the patient listening by all to the conversations going on in the community.

The progressive centralization of the Roman church may be symptomatic of a systemic weakness in the art of listening. Yet African local churches, though greatly weakened by financial dependency, still maintain the claim to the legitimate autonomy of their churches in the communion of churches. The remark by Cardinal Thiandoum in his opening report to the Synod for Africa that the emergence of rites such as that of Zaire is to be considered "as of *right* not as concession" may turn out to be one of the most memorable statements from the synod.

Pastoral Ministry "with Large Ears" and Decentralization

From the evidence it appears that the church of Rome is not finding it easy to fulfill the role of the listening elder brother; she appears to have a long way to go in developing the large ears necessary to create a harmonious and dynamic family. There is no other convincing explanation for the repetition during the African Synod of 1994 of items over which the bishops felt very strongly twenty years earlier. In some ways the voice of the bishops lacked vigor in 1994 compared with the strength of 1974 and 1975. Does this not indicate that our bishops are tired of saying the same thing over and over again without being heard? During the report of three discussion groups in the 1975 SECAM assembly, a strong point was made about the bishops' relationship with the Holy See.

> From their point of view as Pastors, the Bishops find that the Roman procedures take too much time, and seem to belong to another age. To facilitate the work of the apostolate, a decentralization of the Roman services is suggested. However, SECAM must study beforehand what powers it would like to see attributed to the Episcopal Conferences.[60]

Marriage is the dominant issue which has been discussed most frequently by the bishops. During the Sixth Plenary Assembly of SECAM in Yaoundé (Cameroon), from June 29 to July 5, 1981, marriage was discussed in six study commissions and in the general assembly. Among the recommendations and resolutions the African model of the "dynamic progression of the marriage process" came up. There was a recommendation that one should see "how this process could be celebrated in a Christian way and find at what exact moment the canonical form could be inserted, in such a way as to eliminate the present dichotomy between the liturgical and the traditional forms." SECAM recognized also that customs vary from place to place and so "it is for each episcopal conference to make its own practical decisions in a spirit of ecclesial communion."[61] Thirteen years later, on the floor of the Synod for Africa, bishops were again calling for the integration of African customary and Christian marriage (Mgr. Ndingi Mwana'a Nzeki of Kenya and Mgr. E. S. Obot of Nigeria); and the bishops were still expressing concern about the need to give more powers to episcopal conferences to legislate on the same issue of marriage (Mgr. L. A. Sangare of Mali). However, surprisingly, the "Final Proposition" of the African synod, submitted to the pope, sent everyone back to the drawing board.

> We strongly affirm the Church's teaching on the unity and indissolubility of marriage as of divine origin. . . . However, there is the problem of so many Catholics who are being excluded from the sacraments because they have contracted marriage in a form not recognized by the Church. . . . Therefore, the synod recommends that Episcopal Conferences create commissions on Marriage in Africa which will include married couples. Their

aims will be to study all the questions concerning marriage from the point of view of theology, sacramentals, liturgy and canon law with special reference to cultural questions.[62]

I do not think that African bishops are simply to blame for this weak recommendation, which gives the impression that "study commissions" have not agonized over these questions for decades. I think that the relevant departments in Rome must share part of the blame. I am inclined to think that the prevalent attitude of the Roman church toward the African church is like that toward an insignificant congregation within a local community. I have highlighted above the lack of comprehension between Rome and Africa on the issue of inculturation. The overall solution that this study proposes, in order to create real communion among adult sister churches, and without prejudice to the primacy of the see of Peter, is the model of the "listening church," or the apostolate "with large ears."

The first law in this model of pastoral ministry "with large ears," which involves intense listening to the Spirit, who is acknowledged as having initiative within the church and who mediates the attentive listening among all the churches, is real "decentralization." The Vatican bureaucracy compares well with any modern democratic government bureaucracy. But its present pattern of functioning, as an organ which has the answers, is not always helpful for the realization of the church in the African sociocultural area.

When one affirms that the church is the sphere of operation of the Spirit of God, one is acknowledging at the same time the charism of Peter as well as those of the bishops, who are the leaders of the church. The elder brother is confirmed in the task of passing on the ancestral life or patrimony, while his other adult brothers are passing on the same life or patrimony within the various branches of the one ancestral tree. In this respect, pastoral ministry "with large ears" creates a stronger system of freedom at the local church level and enables the one church to bear firm and convincing witness to the Kingdom in the world. The Spirit has full initiative within the church; and the one church confesses the mystery of her oneness realized in the different local churches.

CHAPTER 7

Conclusion: Proposals for the Future

In this book I have drawn attention to the misery that Africans are struggling through. I tried to point out the root historical causes of our distress. The twin unhappy and unparalleled experiences of slavery and colonialism must be lucidly assessed so that we may assume with dignity our history in all its consequences. I do not consider my orientation escapist, as some may believe. Rather, I think it is a realistic way to transcend the evils which dominate us.

The purpose of writing this book is not to bemoan the past. It is neither to blame our tormentors nor to vilify our ancestors. It does not aim at simply denouncing the present political, military, or even ecclesiastical classes, for the way they have abused Africa. Negatively, my purpose is to show that despair does not constitute the basis for the reconstruction of our continent. And positively, my intention is to declare my firm belief in our cultural resources, which constitute the foundation on which we must build the Africa of the future. In view of our defeat by the West, my argument for reconstruction based on our cultural resources is far from being simplistic optimism. It is, rather, a hope based on realism.

African theology drawn fully from a *radical listening* to the gospel, the two-edged sword coming from the mouth of one like the Son of Man (Rev 1:13, 16), and interwoven fully with a *critical retrieval* of our cultural traditions energizes us to propose a way or ways of hearing the Word of the Spirit, of feeling the Wind hovering over our dry bones, our brutalized bodies, our terrorized eyes, and the stinking bowels of our part of this planet earth, full of putrefying corpses of African children, women and men. New life will be created!

In view of our many tears, or the inability to weep any longer (as in Rwanda), I do not propose tears or distress as a point of departure for life in Africa, though we ignore the tears and distress to our own peril. I propose that theology in Africa must assume a ministry of reeducation within an ecclesiology of pedagogy. Paying attention to the groundswell of a burgeoning youth impatient or disdainful of our weak past, misled by the brutality and corruption of our greedy and unimaginative rulers, fascinated by the successful technological culture of the West, but plunging again into a badly digested past tradition in times of distress and oftentimes overpowered by primitive exclusivistic tribal sentiments, Christian theology in Africa may render the invaluable service of introducing an alternative vision in our valuation of life. Christian theology must perform the prophetic ministry of setting a correcting course to life in Africa: *to listen fully in order to release the Word that belongs to the community, the Word that is too large for the mouth of one individual, the Word that heals!*

The path of African theology which I want to thread into this study is that of consciously assuming our history in all its ramifications. Today, this means a way of the cross which is informed by a realistic and eschatological hope that our societies and our lands will be transformed, that our sufferings will come to an end. I neither foresee nor propose the apocalyptic destruction of our enemies, internal or external. This is hardly the ideal of our Christian hope. I, rather, foresee and propose a reconciliation based on linkages, networks, or relationships between peoples, cultures, classes, worlds, and continents. The effective ministry of this reconciliation may lead to the creation of a new earth and a new kind of living based on the humane principle that a human person is human because of other humans.

The focus for the emergence of this new kind of living, in my view and in the view of the authoritative teaching of African bishops and the faithful, is the creation of Small Christian Communities. In the SCCs, at the grassroots level where the initiative belongs to the Spirit of Jesus, the prophetic Word is heard, the community is fully challenged, the contextual problems are fully addressed. This miniature church, which is organized according to the listening model of African tradition, realizes that she does not exist for herself but for the Kingdom, for the transformation of the world.

The prayer and desire of the African bishops in the 1974 Synod on

Evangelization and during the 1994 African Synod are not limited to restructuring the church at the grassroots level alone in order to reflect the relational family model. I argue and propose in this book that the restructuring embraces the totality of the African church. The adoption of the listening model enriches the church through the conversations (or charisms) inspired by the Spirit at all the levels of the People of God—women and men, young and old, poor and rich alike. It is through this listening model, which in political terms may be called consultation, deliberation, or decentralization at all levels, that the church in Africa may be empowered to learn and carry out her vocation in the world of today.

The church may not give what she does not have. Fostering humane living within this family of God energizes her to challenge without fear, to witness even unto death before the tyrannies and dictatorships, the brutalities and massacres, which make many Africans wonder (what blasphemy!) whether God has not really cursed this continent or the black race.

The courage or boldness of the church is clearly testified by the simplicity, service, and caring or mothering of her ministers. A lot depends on leadership. And yet not everything depends on leadership. And precisely because of this, the listening model is the powerful means of empowering the community and its leaders. Ministry is conceived in this study as nonpretentious and nonthreatening. The strength of ministry is testified by the lowliness or weakness of the minister. Ministry becomes the clearest testimony by the church of the creation of an alternative society which distances itself from rank and privilege, abuse and the arrogant exercise of power by military dictators and dictatorships of one-party states.

Courage, Commitment, Conversion

When life gets tough in the Igbo communities of Nigeria, when major interests, objectives, or purposes of life are under threat, my people talk about "swallowing one's life in one's stomach" (*ino ndu na-afo*), burying one's life in one's stomach. Or as the late Professor Donatus Nwoga put it during a popular lecture, during such periods of crisis the cry resounds *eji ndu eme gini! eji ndu eme gini!* (What is life worth!). People sally forth, abandon cherished property, abandon the security of their homes, expose their flanks, put their lives on the line, and die in order to realize the higher motives on which society is founded.

Africa has come to such a crossroads! The most sacred sanctuaries of value and meaning are being eroded by criminal manipulators, military mafiosi, and archaic propagators of an authoritarianism which holds the Spirit of life captive. The cry "Of what worth is life!" must publicly resound as a cry of open, frank, bold witness—the boldness (*parrhesia*) of the renewed Israel of God, the boldness that marks the "companions of Jesus" (Acts 4:13).

For the church in Africa to be an agent of social transformation, she must begin by courageously changing her structures from the inside: "What is life worth!" In order to liberate the Spirit of life, to allow the Spirit initiative in the life of the church-community, this structural change is imperative. The dominance of the Spirit renews the levels or structures of communication and reinvigorates relational channels of communication.

The boldness of the renewed community becomes a conversion of the whole church. It is not only an operation that happens in limited numbers of SCCs made up mainly of the poor and deprived classes. It is the conversion of the church into the little ones (*mikroi*—Mt 10:42; 18:6, 10, 14), where rank and privilege disappear, where primitive sentiments of ethnocentrism or tribalism do not determine the appointment of bishops in Rwanda, Burundi, Nigeria and other countries, where service (*diakonia*) is the overriding rule of ministry. It is the conversion of the church leadership: to look with horror on clericalism and clerical privilege; to look with horror on discriminating against the weak, especially women; to fully put into practice that "there is no longer Jew or Greek, no longer slave or free, no longer male or female" because all "are one in Christ Jesus" (Gal 3:28).

"Of what worth is life!" The church in Africa in her youthfulness is liberated by the Spirit of Jesus to assume responsibility for her witness to the Kingdom. She will not be frightened by the threat of an authoritarian model prevalent in the Western patriarchate. She will not be frightened by the elimination of financial support from a particular sector of the Western church. She will, rather, bring the wealth of her youthful relational experience of the exercise of authority into the communion of churches. As issues of liberation have become part of the experience of the world church, the church in Africa may project onto the world church issues of listening and hearing the other, issues of being related to the other: *Mmotho ke mothoka batho ka bang* (A church is a church because of other churches). There is no question of superior and inferior churches. This relational principle, sharpened by the listening model, may enrich the universal communion of churches to confront the violence, domination, dictatorships, and oppression which are today weighing on the world community.

The church does not exist for herself. She is not an inward-looking organization. She exists to live and proclaim the Kingdom. This Kingdom spreads through her witness especially by creating humane relational channels (*concordia* according to Cyprian of Carthage) that make up the one church of Christ. The experience of our African sociocultural area suggests a renewal of the structures of the church through *listening and hearing the other*, through consultation and deliberation, through real decentralization. The model is not strange, though it may be difficult in these days of overcentralization. It is very close to the New Testament experience. It may be said to have been drawn from the heart of the Master's prescription. It was even practiced in the North African church of Cyprian of Carthage. It will realize the Master's beautiful, humane injunction of love, through which the one church of Jesus Christ is recognized all over the world.

Notes

1. African Reality and African Theology

1. See *L'état du monde, édition 1993: Annuaire économique et géopolitique mondial*, Paris: Éditions La Découverte. See the statistics about Africa, esp. pp. 246-322.

2. See the important contribution of Kä Mana to this debate in his *Théologie africaine pour temps de crise: Christianisme et reconstruction de l'Afrique*, Paris: Karthala, 1993. See also J.-M. Éla, *Le cri de l'homme africain*, Paris: L'Harmattan, 1980; idem, *Afrique: L'irruption des pauvres*, Paris: L'Harmattan, 1994.

3. N. Ndiokwere, *Search for Security*, Enugu: SNAAP Press, 1990; A. Shorter, *Jesus and the Witch Doctor: An Approach to Healing and Wholeness*, London: Chapman, 1985; G. Ludwar-Ene, ed., *New Religious Movements and Society in Nigeria*, Bayreuth, Germany, Bayreuth African Studies Series 17, 1991.

4. For a detailed reappraisal of colonial history from the perspective of the vanquished instead of the victors, see A. Adu Boahen, ed., *General History of Africa*, Vol. 7, *Africa under Colonial Domination, 1880-1935*, UNESCO: 1985; London and Berkeley, California: Heinemann and University of California Press, 1985. The volumes of L. H. Gann and P. Duigan, eds., *Colonialism in Africa, 1870-1960*, vols. 1 and 2, Cambridge: Cambridge University Press, 1969-1970, despite their value were written from the perspective of the victors.

5. Cited by A. Adu Boahen, "Colonialism in Africa: Its Impact and Significance," in Boahen, p. 784.

6. See, for example, B. Bujo, *African Theology in Its Social Context*, Maryknoll, New York: Orbis Books, 1992, pp. 49-73; A. Ngindu Mushete, *Les thèmes majeures de la théologie africaine*, Paris: L'Harmattan, 1989, pp. 11-64; O. Bimwenyi-Kweshi, *Discours théologique négro-africain*, Paris: Présence Africaine, 1981; E. Messi-Metogo, *Théologie africaine ou ethnophilosophie*, Paris: L'Harmattan, 1985.

154

7. During the 1974 synod of bishops the African bishops participating in the synod made a clear option for a "theology of incarnation" in Africa. See their declaration "Promouvoir l'evangélisation dans la coresponsabilitié," *Documentation Catholique,* no. 1665, Nov. 17, 1974, pp. 995-996.

8. See a recent issue of *Concilium* [1994/2], which reexamines the concept and gives examples of the realization of inculturation in various parts of the Christian church. Many interesting works have been done in this direction. See, for example, A. Shorter, *Towards a Theology of Inculturation,* London: Chapman, 1988; A. Peelman, *L'inculturation: L'eglise et les cultures,* Paris: Desclée; Ottawa: Novalis, 1988; N. I. Ndiokwere, *The African Church Today and Tomorrow,* Enugu: SNAAP Press, 1994, 2 vols.

9. O. Obasanjo and A. Mabogunje, eds., *Elements of Democracy,* Abeokuta, Nigeria: ALF Publications, 1992. See the review of this book by O. Iwuchukwu in *Bulletin of Ecumenical Theology,* 5/2: 1993, 71-74.

10. F. Eboussi Boulaga, *Les conférences nationales en Afrique noire: Une affaire à suivre,* Paris: Karthala, 1993; H. Kamgang, *Au-delà de la conférence nationale: Pour les États-unis d'Afrique,* Paris: L'Harmattan, 1993. See my review of Eboussi's book in *Bulletin of Ecumenical Theology,* 5/2: 199, 64-71. I also reviewed Kamgang's book in *Spiritus,* no. 136, Sept. 1994, pp. 365-366.

11. Vatican II, *Constitution on the Sacred Liturgy,* no. 41. All citations of Vatican II are taken from W. M. Abbott, gen. ed., *The Documents of Vatican II,* London: Geoffrey Chapman, 1967.

2. Traditional Institutions of Africa Encounter the West

1. For a general review of the traditional political organizations in Africa, see P. Daigne, *Pouvoir politique traditionnel en Afrique occidentale,* Paris: Présence Africaine, 1967; M. Fortes and E. E. Evans-Pritchard, *African Political Systems,* Oxford: Oxford University Press, 1961; R. Olaniyan, *African History and Culture,* London: Longman, 1982; T. O. Odetola et al., *Man and Society in Africa,* London: Longman, 1983; D. T. Niane, ed., *General History of Africa,* Vol. 4, *Africa from the Twelfth to the Sixteenth Century,* UNESCO, 1984; B. Ogot, ed., *General History of Africa,* Vol. 5, *Africa from the Sixteenth to the Eighteenth Century,* UNESCO, 1992.

2. See Daigne, pp. 21-31, 253-284; Odetola, pp. 52-56.

3. We already indicated the divergencies in practices among the multiple ethnic groups in Africa. While ancestral cults are entrenched in all corners of Africa, there are some societies (like the Tiv of Nigeria) which lack such cults, preferring the direct cult of God or the divinities. In other words, instead of honoring ancestors through prayer, libations and invocations, and instead of having them as mediators between humans and the divine, *Aondo* (Tiv) or

Ngai (Gikuyu) receive direct invocations, prayers and sacrifices from humans.

4. Among the numerous studies of slavery see the two volumes edited by S. Daget, *De la traite à l'esclavage,* Actes du Colloque international sur la Traite des Noirs, Nantes, 1985, Paris: Société Française d' Histoire d'Outre-Mer; Nantes: Centre de Recherche sur l'Histoire du Monde Atlantique, 1988.

5. Cited by G. Gutiérrez, *Las Casas: In Search of the Poor of Jesus Christ,* Maryknoll, New York: Orbis, 1993, p. 327. Gutiérrez tries to correct the mis-understanding of the role of Las Casas in the inhuman slave trade; see especially pp. 319-330.

6. J. Mansi, *Sacrorum Conciliorum Nova et Amplissima Collectio,* vol. 53, col. 634-637, cited by J. Lécuyer, "Libermann et la malédiction de Cham," in P. Coulon et al., *Libermann (1802-1852),* Paris: Cerf, 1988, pp. 596-608.

7. E. Mveng, "Négritude et civilisation gréco-romaine," in *Colloque sur la négritude,* Dakar, Senegal, April 12-18, 1971, Paris: Présence Africaine, 1971, pp. 43-52. On pages 46 and 47 Mveng discusses the quarrel recorded in Numbers, ch. 12, between Moses and his sister Miriam because he had taken to wife a black woman.

8. See John Paul II, "De ce sanctuaire africain de la douleur noire, nous implorons pardon," *Documentation Catholique,* no. 2047, April 5, 1992, pp. 324-325.

9. K. O. Dike, *Trade and Politics in the Niger Delta,* London: Oxford University Press, 1956, p. 114.

10. Chinweizu, *The West and the Rest of Us,* London and Lagos: NOK Publishers, 1978, p. 54.

11. See A. Onwuejeogwu, *An Igbo Civilization: Nri Kingdom and Hegemony,* London: Ethnographica, 1981, p. 28; for the testimony of Nri neighbors about slavery see E. Isichei, *Igbo Worlds: An Anthology of Oral Histories and Historical Descriptions,* London: Macmillan, 1977, pp. 30-34.

12. See J. M. Éla, *De l'assistance à la libération: Les tâches de l'Eglise en milieu africain,* Paris: Centre Lebret, 1981; idem, *Quand l'etat Pénètre en brousse,* Paris: Karthala, 1990; Kä Mana, *Théologie africaine pour temps de crise;* idem, *Christ d'Afrique: Enjeux éthiques de la foi africaine en Jésus-Christ,* Paris: Karthala, 1994.

13. See J. H. Cone, *Martin & Malcolm & America,* London: Fount, 1993, esp. chapter 5; B. Chenu, *Théologies chrétiennes des tiers mondes,* Paris: Centurion, 1987, chapter 2.

14. A. Margarido, "Béatrice du Congo," in Ch. A. Julien et al. eds., *Les Africains,* vol. 9, Paris: Edition Jeune Afrique, 1977, p. 59.

15. See, for example, the interpretation of this phenomenon by A. Mbembe, *Afriques indociles: Christianisme, pouvoir, et état en société postcoloniale,* Paris: Karthala, 1988; and also his "Mourir en post-colonie: Préalables socio-historiques à une théologie africaine de la mort," in J. Doré, R. Luneau, and F.

Kabasele eds., *Pâques africaines d'aujourd'hui*, Paris: Desclée, 1989, pp. 123-130.

16. See Cone, p. 10, quoting from Martin R. Delany, *The Condition, Elevation, Emigration, and Destiny of the Colored People of the United States* (1852).

17. See V. Y. Mudimbe, *The Invention of Africa: Gnosis, Philosophy, and the Order of Knowledge*, Bloomington and Indianapolis: Indiana University Press, 1988; E. Mveng, *L'Afrique dans l'Eglise: Parole d'un croyant*, Paris: L'Harmattan, 1985.

18. D. Richards, "The Ideology of European Dominance," *Présence Africaine*, no. 111, 1979, 3-18, cautions against the linear evolutionary anthropological and colonialist studies of African societies.

19. See L. V. Thomas and R. Luneau, *La terre africaine et ses religions*, Paris: L'Harmattan, p. 9.

20. *Iliad* I, 422-433 cited by C. A. Diop, *Nations nègres et cultures*, Paris: Présence Africaine, 1954, p. 48.

21. Diop, p. 40.

22. See Onwuejeogwu's second interview with Nwaokoye Odenigbo in Isichei, *Igbo Worlds*, pp. 27-28. Okoli Ijeoma, who was a native of Ikelionwu near Awka, used Abam mercenaries (Ada people) to wage war in order to capture slaves (ibid, pp. 104-107).

3. The Reconstruction of African Societies and Church on the Principles of Democracy and Human Rights

1. In *Christ d'Afrique*, Kä Mana challenges the church to bear a credible witness to the gospel in the context of Africa.

2. P. K. Sarpong, "The Individual, Community, Health, and Medicine in African Traditional Religion: The Asante Model," *Pontificium Consilium pro Dialogo inter Religiones Bulletin* 28/3: 1993, 271-280. See also the collective work on the notion of person in Africa, *La notion de la personne en Afrique noire*, Colloques internationaux de CNRS no. 544, Paris, Oct. 11-17, 1971, Paris: CNRS, 1981. For the notion of person among the Igbo see my "Igbo World and Ultimate Reality and Meaning," *Ultimate Reality and Meaning* 5/3: 1982, 188-209; see also E. I. Metuh, *African Religion in Western Conceptual Schemes*, Ibadan: Pastoral Institute, 1985, chapter 7; V. C. Uchendu, *The Igbo of South-eastern Nigeria*, New York: Rinehart and Winston, 1965.

3. A. Boesak, "Le courage et la fierté d'être noire," in A.-M. Goguel et P. Buis, eds., *Chrétiens d'Afrique du sud face à l'apartheid*, Paris: L'Harmattan, 1978, p. 262.

4. Cited by Cone, p. 80.

5. Cited by F. K. Ekechi, *Missionary Enterprise and Rivalry in Igboland*

1857-1914, London: Frank Cass, 1971, p. 37.

6. See ibid., chapter 2.

7. See P. P. Gossiaux, "Mythe et pouvoir—le culte de Ryangombe-Kiranga (Afrique équatoriale de l'est)," in H. Limet et J. Ries, eds., *Le mythe: Son langage et son message,* Actes du Colloque de Liège et Louvain-la-Neuve, 1981, Louvain-la-Neuve: Centre d'Histoire des Religions, 1983, pp. 337-372. See also M.-J. Agossou, *Christianisme africain: Une fraternité au-delà de l'ethnie,* Paris: Karthala, 1987.

8. H. A. Mwanzi, "African Initiatives and Resistance in East Africa, 1880-1914," in Boahen, pp. 149-168, esp. pp. 167-168. See also in the same volume K. A. Opoku, "Religion in Africa during the Colonial Era," esp. pp. 513ff.

9. See Kamgang's plea for and dream of a united Africa on pp. 159-198.

10. See A. Guggenberger, "Personne," in *Encyclopédie de la foi,* vol. 3, Paris: Cerf, 1966, pp. 425-437; also P. Foulquié and R. Saint-Jean, "Personne," in *Dictionnaire de langue philosophique,* Paris: Presses Universitaires de France, 1962; M. Muller and A. Halder, "Person," in K. Rahner, ed., *Encyclopaedia of Theology,* New York: Seabury, 1975, pp. 1206-1213.

11. R. N. Bellah et al., *Habits of the Heart: Individualism and Commitment in American Life,* Berkeley, Calif.: University of California Press, 1985; 1986 edition by New York: Perennial Library, p. 6, esp. chapter 6.

12. See A. F. Walls, "Culture and Coherence in Christian History," *Scottish Bulletin of Evangelical Theology* 3/1: 1985, 5.

13. See G. Lohfink, *L'Eglise que voulait Jésus,* Paris: Cerf, 1985, pp. 13-17; P. Tillich studies the church as "spiritual community" in vol. 3 of his *Systematic Theology,* Chicago: University of Chicago Press, 1963.

4. The Church as Highest Testimony of the Renewal of the Earth

1. Synodus Episcoporum, Coetus Specialis pro Africa, *Nuntius,* Vatican City, 1994, no. 25.

2. See the detailed analysis of Jn 19: 31-34 in M.-E. Boismard and A. Lamouille with G. Rochais, *L'Evangile de Jean,* Paris: Cerf, 1977, pp. 444-452. See also R. Brown, *The Gospel according to John XIII-XXI,* New York: Doubleday, Anchor Bible, 1970, pp. 930-931, 944-952; R. Schnackenburg, *The Gospel according to St John,* vol. 3, London: Burns and Oates, 1982, pp. 284-285, 289-290.

3. See the analysis of this and similar texts by L.-M. Chauvet, *Du symbolique au symbole,* Paris: Cerf, 1979; see also H. Cousin, *L'Evangile de Luc,* Paris: Centurion, 1993, pp. 322-332.

4. See R. Schnackenburg, *The Gospel according to St John,* vol. 1, *Introduction and Commentary on Chapters 1-4,* trans. K. Smyth, London: Burns

and Oates, 1968, pp. 454-458. See also the interesting thesis of T. Okure, *The Johannine Approach to Mission: A Contextual Study of John 4:1-42*, Tübingen: Mohr/Siebeck, 1988.

5. See, for example, J. D. G. Dunn, *Baptism in the Holy Spirit*, London: SCM, 1973.

6. See the interesting commentary on Acts 10:1-11:18 by E. Haenchen, *The Acts of the Apostles: A Commentary*, London: Basil Blackwell, 1971, pp. 343-363. See also E. Haulotte, "Fondation d'une communauté de type universel: Actes 10, 1-11, 18," *Recherches de Science Religieuse* 58: 1970, 63-100.

7. Cyprian, *The Unity of the Catholic Church*, no. 5. See Cyprian, *De Lapsis and De Ecclesiae Catholicae Unitate*, ed. and trans. M. Bénevot, Oxford: Clarendon, 1971.

8. R. E. Brown, "New Testament Background for the Concept of Local Church," in *Proceedings of the 36th Annual Convention of the Catholic Theological Society of America*, June 10-13, 1981, 36: 1982, 1-14 (8-9); and his detailed and suggestive description of the ecclesiologies of these churches in *The Churches the Apostles Left Behind*, New York: Paulist Press, 1984. See also W. A. Meeks, *The First Urban Christians*, New Haven: Yale University Press, 1983.

9. C. Vogel, "Unité de l'Eglise et pluralité des formes historiques d'organisation ecclésiastique du 3e au 5e siècle," in Y. Congar and B.-D. Dupuy, *L'episcopat et l'Eglise universelle*, Paris: Cerf, 1962, p. 601.

10. Cyprian's opening statement "Sententiae Episcoporum Proem," in *Acts of the Seventh Council of Carthage*, Proem, 599a, in *The Faith of the Early Fathers*, vol. 1, trans. W. E. Jurgens, Collegeville: Liturgical Press, 1970, p. 240. See also J. P. Brisson, *Autonomisme et christianisme dans l'Afrique romaine, de Septime Sévère à l'invasion vandale*, Paris: Edition E. de Boccard, 1958, p. 114, note 6; Y. Congar, *Diversité et communion*, Paris: Cerf, 1982, p. 38. The liberty of each bishop and his responsibility before God is clearly stated in Cyprian's Letter 55; see Saint Cyprian, *Correspondence*, trans. le Chanoine Bayard, Paris: Les Belles Lettres, 1925.

11. See Cyprian, *The Unity of the Catholic Church*, nos. 4-5; and Brisson, pp. 59-77.

12. See the critical analysis of the position of Cyprian and the North African church on *concordia* in Brisson, esp. pp. 43-58.

13. See Vogel, p. 605; Hippolytus, *Apostolic Traditions*, chapter 2.

14. Cyprian, Letter 71; see Brisson, pp. 70-72.

15. See C. Munier, "Un canon inédit du XXe Concile de Carthage: 'Ut nullus ad Romanam Ecclesiam audeat appellare,' " *Revue des Sciences Religieuses* 40: 1966, 113-126.

16. J. J. von Allmen, cited by Y. Congar, "Le pape comme patriarche

d'occident: Approche d'une réalité trop négligée," *Istine* 28/4: 1983, 376-390 (pp. 380-381). See also Y. Congar, *L'ecclésiologie du haut Moyen-Age: De saint Grégoire le Grand à la désunion entre Byzance et Rome,* Paris: Cerf, 1968, esp. pp. 131-151; G. Thils, "Le ministère de Pierre et le service de l' 'unité universelle,' " *Révue Théologique de Louvain* 17: 1986, 61-68.

17. Synodus Episcoporum, *Bulletin,* Bureau de Presse du Saint-Siège, April 11, 1994, no. 5, p. 7.

18. J. Ratzinger, "Primat und episcopat," in *Das neue Volk Gottes: Entwürfe zur Ekkesiologie,* cited by Congar, "Le pape comme patriarche d'occident," p. 380.

19. Cyprian, letter 66:8.3.

20. Vatican II, *Constitution on the Liturgy,* no. 41.

21. For these interventions of Paul VI see "Discours pour la clôture du synode," Oct. 26, 1974, *Documentation Catholique,* no. 1664, Nov. 17, 1974, p. 953; "Allocution au Symposium des Conférences épiscopales d'Afrique et de Madagascar," Sept. 26, 1975, *Documentation Catholique,* no. 1684, Oct. 19, 1975, pp. 853-854. The intervention of the bishops of Africa in the 1974 synod is entitled "Promouvoir l'evangélisation dans la coresponsabilité."

22. Congregation for Divine Worship and the Discipline of the Sacraments, "The Roman Liturgy and Inculturation: IVth Instruction for the Right Application of the Conciliar Constitution on the Liturgy (nn. 37-40)," *L'Osservatore Romano,* Weekly Edition, no. 14, April 6, 1994; *Documentation Catholique,* no. 2039, May 1, 1994, pp. 435-446.

23. See, for example, the collection *Liturgie de l'Eglise particulére et liturgie de l'Eglise universelle,* Conférence Saint Serge, XXIIe semaine d'études liturgiques, Paris, June 30-July 3, 1975, Rome: Edizioni Liturgiche, 1976.

24. For the relevant speeches of John Paul II see "Discours aux evêques," May 7, 1980, Nairobi, *Documentation Catholique,* no. 1787, June 1, 1980, pp. 532-535; "La rencontre avec les evêques du Zaïre," Kinshasa, May 3, 1980, *Documentation Catholique,* no. 1787, June 1, 1980, pp. 504-507. For my review of the difficulties in the interpretation of inculturation see my "Le dialogue inter-religieux et l'inculturation du christianisme: Le cas de l'Afrique," a paper delivered at the Institut Catholique de Paris, Feb. 23, 1994, and published in *Revue de l'Institut Catholique de Paris,* no. 51. July-Sept. 1994, pp. 21-42.

5. The "Church-Family"

1. Cyprian, Letter 74:7.2.

2. Lohfink, pp. 54-59, p. 54.

3. Synodus Episcoporum, Coetus Specialis pro Africa, *Elenchus Finalis*

Propositionum, Vatican City, 1994, no. 8.

4. Ibid.

5. See Lohfink, pp. 29-32, 49-54, 177-182.

6. Lohfink assembled a score of passages from Paul where the practice of mutuality characterizes the life of the new Israel of God (ibid., pp. 107-113).

7. Ibid., p. 163; Ignatius of Antioch, *Letter to the Romans,* in the opening address: "Ignatius, also called Theophorus, . . . to the church beloved and enlightened after the love of Jesus Christ . . . to the Church also which holds the presidency in the place of the country of the Romans, worthy of God, worthy of honor, worthy of blessing, worthy of praise, worthy of success, worthy of sanctification, and, because you hold the presidency of love, named after Christ and named after the Father. . . ." Translation from W. A. Jurgens, *The Faith of the Early Fathers,* vol. 1, Collegeville, Minn.: Liturgical Press, 1970, p. 21.

8. See P. Vallely, *Bad Samaritans: First World Ethics and Third World Debt,* Maryknoll, New York: Orbis Books, 1990.

9. See Bellah et al., p. 43.

10. Publication distributed by Church-Business Discussion Group, Zurich, 2nd ed., 1983.

11. See Africa Faith and Justice Network, *Africa Faces Democracy,* Proceedings, Annual Meeting, 1993, Washington, D.C.: Africa Faith and Justice Network, 1994. Information about the network is on the overleaf of the cover.

12. Tertullian, *De Idolatria,* 19; Origen, *Contra Celsum,* 8.73; see Lohfink, pp. 170-182.

13. Synodus Episcoporum, *Nuntius,* no. 25.

14. Bellah et al., pp. 138-139, 154-155.

15. Signed by the European Members of Initiative Kindugu, original text published by *New People,* no. 29, March-April 1994, p. 11.

16. Published in the May-June 1994 issue of *Africa Justice Network.* In the "Message to the People of God," no. 41, the 1994 synod declared, "Together with the Holy Father and the Pontifical Council for Justice and Peace, we ask for at least a substantial, if not a total, remission of the debt."

17. J. Mihevc, "The Theology of Structural Adjustment," *Bulletin of Ecumenical Theology,* 5/1: 1993, 44-60.

18. See *CIIR News,* June 1994, pp. 1, 10-11. See also Africa Faith and Justice Network, Issue Papers, *Fifty Years Is Enough: Anniversary or Jubilee?* June 1994.

19. See Paul VI, *Octogesima Adveniens,* no. 4.

20. P. Kalilombe has done an interesting study of the whole debate on self-reliance and a moratorium. See his "Self-reliance of the African Church: A Catholic Perspective," in Kofi Appiah-Kubi and Sergio Torres, *African Theology en Route,* Maryknoll, New York: Orbis Books, 1979, pp. 36-58.

21. F. Eboussi-Boulaga, "La démission," *Spiritus*, 56: 1974, 276-288.

22. No. 14, as in *L'Osservatore Romano*, Weekly Edition, no. 16, April 20, 1994, p. 10.

23. H. Maurier, *Les missions—religions et civilisations confrontées à l'universalisme: Contribution à une histoire en cours*, Paris: Cerf, 1993, p. 43.

24. B. Carr, "The Mission of the Moratorium," cited by C. B. Okolo, *The Liberation Role of the Church in Africa Today*, Eldoret: Gaba Publications, Spearhead 119, 1991, p. 42. The issue of the moratorium was raised during the Third Assembly of the All Africa Conference of Churches, in Lusaka, Zambia, May 1974. Burgess Carr expressed his views on the problems facing the Christian churches in Africa in his keynote address: "The Engagement of Lusaka," IDOC Bulletin, n. 22, August 1974, pp. 2-10.

25. Synodus Episcoporum, *Elenchus Finalis Propositionum*, no. 16.

26. G. Kembo Mamputu's intervention during the synod for Africa, "Our Populations lie in Poverty and Misery," *L'Osservatore Romano*, Weekly Edition, no. 19, May 11, 1994, p. 12.

27. P. Johnson, *A History of Christianity*, London: Penguin Books, 1976, pp. 148-152. See also R. Pernoud, J. Gimpel, and R. Delatouche, *Le Moyen Age pour quoi faire?* Paris: Editions Stock, 1986, especially the paragraph "Si le tiers monde avait eu des cisterciens," pp. 301-303.

28. Archbishop Charles Vandame, "Ecclesial Communities and Financial Dependence," *L'Osservatore Romano*, Weekly Edition, no. 20, May 18, 1994, p. 8.

29. J. Diop-Yansunnu, "The Life and Formation of Priests," *L'Osservatore Romano*, Weekly Edition, no. 21, May 25, 1994, p. 5.

30. Archbishop Jean Zoa, "Synod Listens to Africa," *L'Osservatore Romano*, no. 17, April 27, 1994, p. 10.

31. See P. Freire, *Pedagogy of the Oppressed*, New York: Seabury, 1970, pp. 100-101.

32. Vatican II, *Apostolicam Actuositatem*, no. 7; *Lumen Gentium*, no. 31. See the address of Bishop C. Mwoleka to the SECAM meeting in Rome, 1975, "The Two Forms of Evangelization Demanded by Our Time: Small Christian Communities and Human Promotion," in *Acts of the Fourth Plenary Assembly of the Symposium of the Episcopal Conferences of Africa and Madagascar*, Rome, 1975, pp. 172-188, especially pp. 181-188.

33. A. Tsiahoana, "The Formation of Malagasy Priests," *L'Osservatore Romano*, Weekly Edition, no. 17, April 27, 1994, p. 9.

6. Service in the African Church

1. See Synodus Episcoporum, *Elenchus Finalis Propositionum*, no. 18;

and the intervention of Bishop Michael Cleary of Banjul, Gambia, in *L'Osservatore Romano*, Weekly Edition, no. 17, April 27, 1994, p. 11.

2. A. T. Sanon, "The Church Is Communion, Family, and Brotherhood," *L'Osservatore Romano*, Weekly Edition, no. 17, April 27, 1994, p. 14.

3. C. Achebe, "*Chi* in Igbo Cosmology," in *Morning Yet on Creation Day: Essays*, London: Heinemann, 1975, p. 98.

4. Synodus Episcoporum, *Elenchus Finalis Propositionum*, no. 8.

5. "Relatio post Disceptationem," April 22, 1994, in *L'Osservatore Romano*, Weekly Edition, no. 21, May 25, 1994, p. 9.

6. Vatican II, *Dogmatic Constitution on the Church*, chapter 2.

7. I argue this in detail in "Body and Memory in African Liturgy," *Concilium*, 1995/3, pp. 71-78.

8. G. Philips, *L'Eglise et son mystère au IIe Concile du Vatican*, Vol. 1, Tournai: Desclée, 1967, p. 7, cited by G. Thils, "Le nouveau code de droit canonique et l'ecclesiologie de Vatican II," *Revue Théologique de Louvain* 14: 1983, p. 299.

9. Sanon, p. 14.

10. AMECEA Bishops, "Planning for the Church in Eastern Africa in the 1980s," *African Ecclesial Review* 16/1 and 2, 1974.

11. Quote taken from the report of Archbishop J. Zoa to the 1975 SECAM meeting held in Rome, "A Panoramic Approach of the 1974 Synod," in *Acts of the Fourth Plenary Assembly of SECAM*, Accra: SECAM Secretariat, 1975, p. 73.

12. *Acts of the Fourth Plenary Assembly of the SECAM*, pp. 296-297.

13. In A. Radoli, ed., *How Local Is the Local Church? Small Christian Communities and Church in East Africa*, Eldoret, Kenya: AMECEA Gaba Publications, Spearhead, nos. 126-128, 1993.

14. L. J. Lebulu, "A Pastoral Action for Development," *L'Osservatore Romano*, Weekly Edition, no. 19, May 11, 1994, p. 12.

15. Mwoleka, pp. 173-174.

16. Citation from J. G. Healey, "Twelve Case Studies of Small Christian Communities (SCCs) in Eastern Africa," in Radoli, pp. 65-66.

17. F. J. Silota, "Living the Christian Message in 'African Communitarianism,' " *L'Osservatore Romano*, Weekly Edition, no. 18, May 4, 1994, p. 12.

18. A. Mayala, "The Laity and the Proclamation of the Word," *L'Osservatore Romano*, Weekly Edition, no. 18, May 4, 1994, p. 10.

19. M. Weber, *The Sociology of Religion*, Boston: Beacon Press, 1963, esp. chapters 6-8; see also J. G. Gager, *Kingdom and Community: The Social World of Early Christianity*, Englewood Cliffs, New Jersey: Prentice-Hall, 1975, pp. 97-101.

20. Healey, "Twelve Case Studies of Small Christian Communities," p. 78.

21. *Acts of the Fourth Plenary Assembly of SECAM*, p. 237.

22. Magesa, "The Church in Eastern Africa, Retrospect and Prospect," p. 7; Healey, "Twelve Case Studies of Small Christian Communities," in A. Radioli, ed., *How Local Is the Local Church? Small Christian Communities and Church in East Africa*, p. 79.

23. J. G. Healey, "Four Africans Evaluate S.C.C.s in E. Africa," *African Ecclesial Review* 29/5: 1987, 266-277. The summary is taken from my "The Birth and Development of a Local Church: Difficulties and Signs of Hope," *Concilium* 1992/1, p. 18.

24. C. Mwoleka, pp. 181-182.

25. Pius X, *Vehementer Nos*, 1906, no. 8. See *Encyclical of Pope Pius X on the French Law of Separation*, in *The Papal Encyclicals 1903-1939*, New York: McGrath, 1981.

26. See Y. Congar, *Lay People in the Church*, London: Geoffrey Chapman, 1965.

27. L. Boff, *Church, Charism and Power: Liberation Theology and the Institutional Church*, New York: Crossroad, 1986, pp. 40-41.

28. Pius X, *Vehementer Nos*, no. 8.

29. The issue of democratization is very well handled in its ramifications by E. Schillebeeckx, *Church: The Human Story of God*, New York: Crossroad, 1990, chapter 4.

30. Cyprian, Letter 66:8.3.

31. See Cyprian, Letters 3:2; 65:2.

32. Cyprian, Letter 67: 4-5; see also P. van Beneden, *Aux origines d'une terminologie sacramentelle: Ordo, ordinare, ordinatio dans la littérature chrétienne avant 313*, Louvain: Spicilegium Sacrum Lovaniense, 1974, p. 147f.

33. J. Ratzinger and H. Maïer, *Démocratisation dans l'Eglise? Possibilités, limites, risques*, Paris: Apostolat; Quebec: Paulines, 1972, p. 50.

34. *Acta Saturnini*, nos. 9 and 11, *PL* 689ff; see A. Hamman, "La prière chrétienne et la prière païenne, formes et différences," in H. Temporini and W. Haase, eds., *Aufstieg und Niedergang der römischen Welt*, Berlin: Walter der Gruyter, II. 23,2, 1980, pp. 1190-1247, esp. pp. 1207-1208.

35. L. V. Thomas and R. Luneau, *Les religions d'Afrique noire*, Paris: Stock and Plus, 1981, vol. 1, p. 28.

36. See "South Africa: Power to the People?" *West Africa*, April 25-May 1, 1994, p. 718.

37. See archives of the Church Missionary Society, London—CMS G3/A3/0, H. Johnson Report of Stations in the Archdeaconry of the Upper Niger for the Year ending December 1881, cited by F.K. Ekechi, *Missionary Enterprise and Rivalry in Igboland 1857-1914* London: Frank Cass, 1971, p. 46.

38. Tertullian, *On Prescription against Heretics*, ch. 20, in *The Ante-Nicene*

Fathers, vol. 3, trans. and ed. by A. Roberts and J. Donaldson, Edinburgh: T & T Clark, 1989 reprint.

39. Cyprian, Letters 48 (to Cornelius), 66 (to Florentius), 72 (from Cyprian and other Bishops to Stephen of Rome), 75 (from Firmilian to Cyprian)—as in Cyprian, *Correspondence*; see also Beneden, p. 152f.

40. See, for example, X. Léon-Dufour, *Sharing the Eucharistic Bread: The Witness of the New Testament*, New York: Paulist Press, 1987.

41. Teresa Okure, "Leadership in the New Testament," *Nigerian Journal of Theology*, 1/5: 1990, 85-86.

42. M. A. Oduyoye, "Feminist Theology in an African Perspective," in R. Gibellini, ed., *Paths of African Theology*, Maryknoll, New York: Orbis, 1994, pp. 174, 176.

43. E. Schillebeeckx, *Ministry*, New York: Crossroad, 1981, p. 30.

44. K. H. Rengstorf, "apostolos," in G. Kittel, ed., *Theological Dictionary of the New Testament*, vol. 3, Grand Rapids: Eerdmans, 1964, pp. 393-447.

45. Ignatius of Antioch, *Letter to the Romans*, nos. 2 and 4, in *Early Christian Writings: The Apostolic Fathers*, trans. by M. Staniforth, Middlesex, England: Penguin, 1968.

46. The words used for "perfection" and "being perfected"—*teleiôsis* and *teleiôtês*—suggest the ordeal in the initiatory passage. In other words the tests, trials, and sufferings which candidates undergo during the traditional initiation rites in Africa and which transform them into new persons.

47. The description of the Bobo chiefs and leaders of initiation is taken from A. T. Sanon, "Jésus, Maître d'initiation," in J. Doré et al., *Chemins de la christologie africaine*, Paris: Desclée, 1986, pp. 143-166, esp. 146-150.

48. In their "Message to the People of God" the synod Fathers said, "We are convinced that *the quality of our Church-as-Family also depends on the quality of our women-folk, be they married or members of institutes of the consecrated life*" (Synodus Episcoporum, *Nuntius*, no. 68).

49. Ibid, no. 15.

50. Ali A. Mazrui in his introduction to A. A. Mazrui, ed., with C. Wondji, *General History of Africa*, vol. 8, *Africa since 1935*, UNESCO and Berkeley, California: University of California Press, 1993, p. 17.

51. For an interesting study of power as dominance and relational power from a feminist perspective see C. Twohig-Moengangongo, "Paradigms of Power," *Bulletin of Ecumenical Theology* 6/1: 1994, 33-51.

52. A. N. Nasimiya-Wasiki, "The Role of Women in Small Christian Communities," in A. Radoli, p. 187.

53. *Testamentum Domini* is a Syriac document which derives from the third-century *Apostolic Tradition* of Hippolytus. It contains plenty of archaisms, but the final redaction was probably between the fourth and fifth centuries.

54. My comments depend on the study of M. Arranz, "Les rôles dans l'assemblée chrétienne d'après le 'Testamentum Domini,' " in *L'assemblée liturgique et les différents rôles dans l'assemblée*, Conférence Saint-Serge, XXIIIe Semaine d'Etudes liturgiques, Paris, June 28-July 1, 1976. Rome: Edizioni Liturgiche, 1977, pp.43-77, p. 52.

55. *Testamentum Domini*, chapter 41, cited by Arranz, p. 64.

56. Mwoleka, p. 173.

57. B. Bujo, *African Theology in Its Social Context*, Maryknoll, New York: Orbis, 1992, pp. 25-26, 100-103. See also J.-M. R. Tillard, *Church of Churches: The Ecclesiology of Communion*, Collegeville, Minn.: Liturgical Press, 1992, esp. chapter 4, "The Visible Communion of the Churches." My book was already with the publishers before my attention was drawn to the recent and authoritative work of J.-M. R. Tillard on the local Church: *L'Eglise locale. Ecclésiologie de communion et catholicité*. Paris: Cerf, 1995.

58. J. Zoa, "A Panoramic Approach to the 1974 Synod," in *Acts of the Fourth Plenary Assembly of SECAM*, esp. pp. 79-81, 87-88.

59. J. D. Sangu, "SECAM and Evangelisation in Africa," in *Acts of the Fourth Plenary Assembly of SECAM*, p. 103.

60. *Acts of the Fourth Plenary Assembly of SECAM*, p. 221.

61. *Acts of the Sixth Plenary Assembly of the Symposium of Episcopal Conferences of Africa and Madagascar*, Yaoundé, June 29-July 5, 1981, Accra: SECAM Secretariat, 1981, p. 157.

62. Proposition no. 35.

Bibliography

Africa: History, Politics, Economy, Anthropology

Achebe, C. "Chi in Igbo Cosmology," in *Morning Yet on Creation Day: Essays* (London: Heinemann, 1975), pp. 93-103.

Boahen, A. Adu, ed. *General History of Africa*, Vol. 7: *Africa under Colonial Domination, 1880-1935* (London and Berkeley, Calif.: UNESCO, Heinemann and University of California Press, 1985).

Chinweizu. *The West and the Rest of Us* (London and Lagos: NOK Publishers, 1978).

Daget, S., ed. *De la traite à l'esclavage*. Actes du Colloque international sur la Traite des Noirs, Nantes 1985 (Paris: Société Française d'Histoire d'Outre-mer; Nantes: Centre de Recherche sur l'Histoire du Monde Atlantique, 1988).

Daigne, P. *Pouvoir politique traditionnel en Afrique occidentale* (Paris: Présence Africaine, 1967).

Dike, K. O. *Trade and Politics in the Niger Delta* (London: Oxford University Press, 1956).

Diop, C. A. *Nations nègres et cultures* (Paris: Présence Africaine, 1954).

Eboussi-Boulaga, F. *Les conférences nationales en Afrique noire: Une affaire à suivre* (Paris: Karthala, 1993).

Ekechi, F. K. *Missionary Enterprise and Rivalry in Igboland, 1857-1914* (London: Frank Cass, 1971).

Fortes, M., and E. E. Evans-Pritchard. *African Political Systems* (Oxford: Oxford University Press, 1961).

Gann, L. H., and P. Duigan, eds. *Colonialism in Africa, 1870-1960* (Cambridge: Cambridge University Press, 1969-1970, 2 vols.).

Gossiaux, P. P. "Mythe et pouvoir: Le culte de Ryangombe-Kiranga (Afrique équatoriale de l'Est)," in H. Limet and J. Ries, eds., *Le mythe: Son langage et son message*. Actes du Colloque de Liège et Louvain-la-Neuve, 1981 (Louvain-la-Neuve: Centre d'Histoire des Religions, 1983), pp. 337-372.

Isichei, E. *Igbo Worlds: An Anthology of Oral Histories and Historical Descriptions* (London: Macmillan, 1977).

Kamgang, H. *Au-delà de la conférence nationale: Pour les États-unis d'Afrique* (Paris: L'Harmattan, 1993).

L'état du monde: Annuaire économique et géopolitique mondial (Paris: Editions La Découverte, 1993).

Margarido, A. "Béatrice du Congo," in C. A. Julien et al., eds., *Les Africains,* Vol. 9 (Paris: Édition Jeune Afrique, 1977), pp. 47-79.

La notion de la personne en Afrique noire. Colloques internationaux de CNRS no. 544, Oct. 11-17, 1971 (Paris: CNRS, 1981).

Mazrui, A. A. Introduction to *General History of Africa,* Vol. 8: *Africa since 1935,* A. A. Mazrui, ed., with C. Wondji, (London and Berkeley, Calif.: UNESCO, Heinemann and University of California Press, 1993).

Metuh, E. I. *African Religion in Western Conceptual Schemes* (Ibadan: Pastoral Institute, 1985).

Niane, D. T., ed. *General History of Africa* Vol. 4: *Africa from the Twelfth to the Sixteenth Century* (London and Berkeley, Calif.: UNESCO, Heinemann and University of California Press, 1984).

Obasanjo, O., and A. Mabogunje, eds. *Elements of Democracy* (Abeokuta, Nigeria: ALF Publications, 1992).

Odetola, T. O., et al. *Man and Society in Africa* (London: Longman, 1983).

Ogot, B., ed. *General History of Africa,* Vol. 5: *Africa from the Sixteenth to the Eighteenth Century* (London and Berkeley, Calif.: UNESCO, Heinemann and University of California Press, 1992).

Olaniyan, R. *African History and Culture* (London: Longman, 1982).

Onwuejeogwu, A. *An Igbo Civilization: Nri Kingdom and Hegemony* (London: Ethnographica, 1981).

Richards, D. "The Ideology of European Dominance," *Présence Africaine* 111 (1979): 3-18.

"South Africa: Power to the People," in *West Africa* (April 25-May 1, 1994): 718.

Thomas, L. V., and R. Luneau. *La terre africaine et ses religions* (Paris: L'Harmattan, 1980).

———. *Les religions d'Afrique noire,* Vol. 1 (Paris: Stock & Plus, 1981).

Uchendu, V. C. *The Igbo of South-eastern Nigeria* (New York: Rinehart and Winston, 1965).

Uzukwu, E. E. "Igbo World and Ultimate Reality and Meaning," *Ultimate Reality and Meaning* 5/3 (1982): 188-209.

African Theology: Inculturation, Liberation, Black Theology

Adoukonou, B. *Jalons pour une théologie africaine: Essai d'une herméneutique chrétienne du Vodun dahoméen* (Paris: Editions Lethielleux; Dessain et Tolra), 1980, 2 vols.

Agossou, M. J. *Christianisme africain: Une fraternité au-delà l'ethnie* (Paris: Karthala, 1987).

Bimwenyi-Kweshi, O. *Discours théologique négro-africain: Problèmes des fondements* (Paris: Présence Africaine, 1981).

Boesak, A. "Le courage et la fierté d'être noire," in A. M. Goguel and P. Buis, eds., *Chrétiens d'Afrique du sud face à l'apartheid* (Paris: L'Harmattan, 1978), pp. 228-263.

Bujo, B. "Pour une Ethique africano-christocentrique," *Bulletin de Théologie Africaine*, III/5: 1981.

————. *African Theology in Its Social Context* (Maryknoll, New York: Orbis Books and Nairobi: St. Paul Publications, 1992).

Chenu, B. *Théologies chrétiennes des tiers mondes* (Paris: Centurion, 1987).

Cone, J. H. *Martin & Malcom & America* (Maryknoll, New York: Orbis Books; London: Fount, 1993).

Des Prêtres noirs s'interrogent, Paris: Présence Africaine, 1956.

Dimandja, E.K. and S. Mbonyinkebe, (eds.) *Théologie et Cultures. Mélanges offerts à Mgr Alfred Vanneste.* Louvain-la-neuve: Editions Noraf, 1988.

Eboussi Boulaga, F. "La démission," *Spiritus* 56 (1974):276-288.

————. *Christianisme sans Fétiche: Révélations et Domination.* Paris: Présence Africaine, 1981 [English translation *Christianity Without Fetishes,* Maryknoll: Orbis].

————. *A Contretemps: L'Enjeu de Dieu en Afrique.* Paris: Karthala, 1991, surtout pp. 127-153.

Éla, J.-M. *Le Cri de l'homme africain* (Paris: L'Harmattan), 1980 [English translation *African Cry* (Maryknoll, New York: Orbis, 1986)].

————. *De l'assistance à libération: Les tâches de l'Église en milieu africain* (Paris: Centre Lebret, 1981).

————. *Quand l'état pénètre en brousse* (Paris: Karthala, 1990).

————. *Afrique: L'irruption des pauvres* (Paris: L'Harmattan, 1994).

Éla, J.-M. and R. Luneau. *Voici le Temps des Héritiers* (Paris: Karthala, 1981).

Gibellini, R. ed. *Paths of African Theology* (Maryknoll, New York: Orbis, 1994).

Healey, J. G. "Four Africans Evaluate SCCs in E. Africa," *African Ecclesial Review* 29/5 (1987):266-277.

————. "Twelve Case Studies of Small Christian Communities in Eastern Africa," in A. Radoli, ed. *How Local is the Local Church? Small Christian Communities in Eastern Africa* (Eldoret, Kenya: AMACEA Gaba Publications, Spearhead, nos. 126-128, 1993), pp. 59-103.

Hebga, M.P., *Afrique de la Raison, Afrique de la Foi* (Paris: Karthala, 1995).

Kabasélé-Lumbala, J. Doré, et R. Luneau, *Chemins de la Christologie africaine* (Paris: Desclée, 1986). [Adapted by Orbis, *Faces of Christ in Africa* edited by R. Schreiter].

————. *Paques Africaines d'Aujourd'hui.* Paris: Desclée, 1989.

Kabasélé-Lumbala. *Le Christianisme et l'Afrique: Une Chance Réciproque* (Paris: Karthala, 1993).

Kalilombe, P. "Self-Reliance of the African Church: A Catholic Perspective," in Kofi Appiah-Kubi and Sergio Torres, *African Theology en Route* (Maryknoll, New York: Orbis Books, 1979), pp. 36-58.

Kuamba Lufunda, "Impasse d'une théologie de l'inculturation," *Philosophie Africaine face aux Libérations Religieuses.* Actes de la XIe Semaine Philosophique de Kinshasa, du de nov. au 03 déc. 1988 (Facultés Catholiques de Kinshasa, 1990), pp. 199-215.

Magesa, L. "The Church in Eastern Africa: Retrospect and Prospect," in *How Local Is the Local Church? Small Christian Communities in Eastern Africa* (Eldoret, Kenya: AMACEA Gaba Publications, Spearhead, nos. 126-128, 1993), pp. 3-35.

Mana, Kä, *Théologie africaine pour temps de crise: Christianisme et reconstruction de l'Afrique* (Paris: Karthala, 1993).

————. *Christ d'Afrique: Enjeux éthiques de la foi africaine en Jésus-Christ* (Paris: Karthala, 1994).

Maurier, H. *Les missions—religions et civilisations confrontées à l'universalisme: Contribution à une histoire en cours* (Paris: Cerf, 1993).

Mbembe, A. *Afriques indociles: Christianisme, pouvoir, et état en société post-coloniale* (Paris: Karthala, 1988).

————. "Mourir en post-colonie," in J. Doré, R. Luneau, and F. Kabasele, eds., *Pâques africaines d'aujourd'hui* (Paris: Desclée, 1989), pp. 123-130.

Messi-Metogo, E. *Théologie africaine ou ethnophilosophie* (Paris: L'Harmattan, 1985).

Mudimbe, V. Y. *The Invention of Africa: Gnosis, Philosophy, and the Order of Knowledge* (Bloomington and Indianapolis: Indiana University Press, 1988).

Mveng, E. "Négritude et civilization gréco-romaine," in *Colloque sur la négritude* (Paris: Présence Africaine, 1971), pp. 43-52.

————. *L'Afrique dans l'Église: Paroles d'un croyant* (Paris: L'Harmattan, 1985).

————, ed. *Spiritualité et libération en Afrique* (Paris: l'Harmattan, 1989).

Nasimiyu-Wasike, A. N. "The Role of Women in Small Christian Communities," in *How Local Is the Local Church? Small Christian Communities in Eastern Africa* (Eldoret, Kenya: AMACEA Gaba Publications, Spearhead, nos. 126-128, 1993), pp. 181-202.

Ndi-Okalla, J. ed., *Inculturation et Conversion.* Africains et Européens face au Synode des Eglises d'Afrique. Paris: Karthala, 1994.

Ndiokwere, N. *Search for Security* (Enugu: SNAAP Press, 1990).

————. *The African Church Today and Tomorrow: Inculturation in Practice*, Vol. 2 (Enugu: SNAAP Press, 1994).

————. *The African Church Today and Tomorrow: Prospects and Challenges*, Vol. 1 (Enugu: SNAAP Press, 1994).

Ngindu Mushete, A. *Les thèmes majeurs de la théologie africaine* (Paris: L'Harmattan, 1989).

Oduyoye, M. A. "Feminist Theology in an African Perspective," in R. Gibellini, ed., *Paths of African Theology* (Maryknoll, New York: Orbis Books, 1994), pp. 166-181.

Okolo, C. B. *The Liberation Role of the Church in Africa Today* (Eldoret, Kenya: AMACEA Gaba Publications, Spearhead, no. 119, 1991).

Okure, T. *The Johannine Approach to Mission: A Contextual Study of John 4:1-42* (Tübingen: Mohr/Siebeck, 1988).

————. "Leadership in the New Testament," *Nigerian Journal of Theology* 1/5 (1990): 71-93.

Peelman, A. *L'inculturation: L'Eglise et les cultures* (Paris: Desclée; Ottawa: Novalis, 1988).

Radoli, A., ed. *How Local Is the Local Church? Small Christian Communities and Church in Eastern Africa* (Eldoret: AMACEA Gaba Publications, Spearhead, nos. 126-128, 1993).

Sanon, A. T. "Christ," in J. Doré et al., *Chemins de la christologie africaine* (Paris: Desclée, 1986), pp. 143-166; [English translation "Jesus, Master of Initiation," in R. Schreiter, ed. *Faces of Jesus in Africa* (Maryknoll, New York: Orbis Books, 1991), pp. 85-102].

Sarpong P. K., "The Individual, Community, Health, and Medicine in African Traditional Religion: The Asante Model," *Pontificium Consilium pro Dialogo inter Religiones Bulletin* 28/3 (1993):271-280.

Shorter, A. *Jesus and the Witchdoctor: An Approach to Healing and Wholeness* (Maryknoll, New York: Orbis Books; London: Chapman, 1985).

————. *Towards a Theology of Inculturation* (Maryknoll, New York: Orbis Books; London: Chapman, 1988).

Tillard, J.-M. R. *L'Eglise Locale: Ecclésiologie de communion et catholicité* (Paris: Cerf, 1995).

Uzukwu, E. E. "The Birth and Development of a Local Church: Difficulties and Signs of Hope," *Concilium* (1992/1):17-23.

————. "Le dialogue inter-religieux et l'inculturation du christianisme: Le cas de l'Afrique," *Revue de l'Institut Catholique de Paris*, no. 51 (July-Sept. 1994):21-42.

————. "Body and Memory in African Liturgy," *Concilium* (1995/3):71-78.

Church Documents, Declarations, Fathers of the Church

Abbott, W. M., ed. *The Documents of Vatican II* (London: Chapman, 1967).

Acts of the Fourth Plenary Assembly of the Symposium of Episcopal Confer-

ences of Africa and Madagascar, held in Rome, 1975 (Accra, Ghana: SECAM Secretariat, 1975).

Acts of the Sixth Plenary Assembly of the Symposium of Episcopal Conferences of Africa and Madagascar (SECAM), held in Yaoundé, June 29-July 5, 1981 (Accra, Ghana: SECAM Secretariat, 1981).

AMECEA Bishops, "Planning for the Church in Eastern Africa in the 1980s," *African Ecelesial Review* 16/1 and 2 (1974).

Bishops of Africa, "Promouvoir l'évangélisation dans la coresponsabilité," *Documentation Catholique,* no. 1665 (Nov. 17, 1974):995-996.

Cheza, M., H. Derroitte and R. Luneau, eds. *Les évêques d'Afrique parlent (1969-1991)* (Paris: Centurion, 1992).

Congregation for Divine Worship and the Discipline of the Sacraments, "The Roman Liturgy and Inculturation: IVth Instruction for the Right Application of the Conciliar Constitution on the Liturgy (nos. 37-40)," *L'Osservatore Romano,* Weekly Edition, no. 14 (April 6, 1994); also in *Documentation Catholique,* no. 2039 (May 1, 1994):435-446.

Cyprian of Carthage. *Correspondence,* trans. le Chanoine Bayard (Paris: Les Belles Lettres, 1925).

———. "Sententiae Episcoporum Proem" in *Acts of the Seventh Council of Carthage,* Proem 599a, in *The Faith of the Early Fathers,* trans. W. E. Jurgens, Vol. 1., (Collegeville: Liturgical Press, 1970).

———. *De Lapsis and De Ecclesiae Catholicae Unitate,* ed. and trans. M. Bénevot (Oxford; Clarendon, 1971).

Ignatius of Antioch. *Letter to the Romans,* in *The Faith of the Early Fathers,* trans. W. A. Jurgens, Vol. 1 (Collegeville: Liturgical Press, 1970); and *Early Christian Writings: The Apostolic Fathers,* trans. M. Staniforth (Middlesex, England: Penguin, 1968).

John Paul II. "Discours aux évêques" (May 7, 1980, Nairobi), *Documentation Catholique,* no. 1787 (June 1, 1980):532-535.

———. "La rencontre avec les évêques du Zaïre" (May 3, 1980, Kinshasa), *Documentation Catholique,* no. 1787 (June 1, 1980):504-507.

———. "De ce sanctuaire africain de la douleur noire, nous implorons pardon," *Documentation Catholique,* no. 2047 (April 5, 1992), pp. 324-325.

Mansi, J. *Sacrorum Conciliorum Nova et Amplissima Collectio,* Vol. 52.

Mwoleka, C. "The Two Forms of Evangelization Demanded by Our Time: Small Christian Communities and Human Promotion," in *Acts of the Fourth Plenary Assembly of SECAM* held in Rome, 1975:172-188.

"Open Letter from the Bishops of Africa to Our Brother Bishops in Europe and North America" (Washington, D.C.: Africa Faith and Justice Network, May/June, 1994).

Origen. *Contre Celse.* vol. I-vol. V, Source Chrétienne nos. 132, 136, 147,

150, 227 respectively (Paris: Cerf, 1967, 1968, 1969, and 1976).

Paul VI. "Discours pour la clôture du synode" (Oct. 26, 1974), *Documentation Catholique*, no. 1664 (Nov. 17, 1974):953.

———. "Allocution au Symposium des Conférences épiscopales d'Afrique et de Madagascar" (Sept. 26, 1975), *Documentation Catholique*, no. 1684 (Oct. 19, 1975):853-854.

Pius X. *Vehementer Nos* (1906), in *The Encyclical of Pope Pius X on the French Law of Separation: The Papal Encyclicals, 1903-1939* (New York: McGrath, 1981).

Sangu, J. D. "SECAM and Evangelisation in Africa," in *Acts of the Fourth Plenary Assembly of SECAM* held in Rome, 1975:95-105.

Synodus Episcoporum, *Elenchus Finalis Propositionum* (Vatican City, 1994).

Synodus Episcoporum, Coetus Specialis pro Africa, *Nuntius* (Vatican City, 1994).

Tertullian. *De Idolatria.*

———. *On Prescription against Heretics*, in *The Ante-Nicene Fathers*, trans. and ed. by A. Roberts and J. Donaldson, Vol. 3 (Edinburgh: T. & T. Clark, 1989 reprint).

Testamentum Domini Nostri Iesu Christi, ed. I. E. Rahmani (1899; Hildesheim: Georg Olms, 1968 reprint).

Thiandoum, H. "Relatio ante Disceptationem," in Synodus Episcoporum, *Bulletin*, no. 5 (Vatican City: Bureau de Presse du Saint-Siège, April 11, 1994); also in *L'Osservatore Romano* (No. 16, April 20, 1994).

———. "Relatio post Disceptationem," *L'Osservatore Romano* (No. 21, May 25, 1994).

Zoa, J. "A Panoramic View of the 1974 Synod," in *Acts of the Fourth Plenary Assembly of SECAM* held in Rome, 1975:70-94.

[Many interventions of Fathers and participants in the 1994 African synod are cited in this study. Most of these are contained in *L'Osservatore Romano*, Weekly Edition, nos. 15-21 (April 13-May 25, 1994).]

Other Works Relevant to This Study

Africa Faith and Justice Network, *Africa Faces Democracy*. Proceedings, Annual Meeting, 1993 (Washington, D.C.: Africa Faith and Justice Network, 1994).

———. *Fifty Years Is Enough: Anniversary or Jubilee*, Issue Papers. Washington D.C.: AFJN, June 15, 1994.

Arranz, M. "Les rôles dans l'assemblée chrétienne d'après le 'Testamentum Domini,' " in *L'assemblée liturgique et les différents rôles dans l'assemblée*, Conférences Saint-Serge, XXIIIe Semaine d'Etudes liturgiques, Paris, June 28-July 1, 1976 (Rome: Edizioni Liturgiche, 1977), pp. 43-77.

174 BIBLIOGRAPHY

Bellah, R. N., et al. *Habits of the Heart: Individualism and Commitment in American Life* (Berkeley, Calif.: University of California Press, 1985).

Boff, L. *Church—Charism and Power: Liberation Theology and the Institutional Church* (New York: Crossroad, 1986).

Boismard, M. E., and A. Lamouille, with G. Rochais. *L'Evangile de Jean* (Paris: Cerf, 1977).

Brisson, J. P. *Autonomisme et christianisme dans l'Afrique romaine, de Septime Sévère à l'invasion vandale* (Paris: Édition E. de Boccard, 1958).

Brown, R. E. *The Gospel according to John XIII-XXI* (New York: Doubleday, Anchor Bible, 1970).

———. "New Testament Background for the Concept of Local Church," in *Proceedings of the 36th Annual Convention of the Catholic Theological Society of America* 36 (1982):1-14.

———. *The Churches the Apostles Left Behind* (New York: Paulist Press, 1984).

Catholic Institute for International Relations (CIIR). *Fifty Years Is Enough,* London: CIIR, June 1994, pp. 1, 10-11.

Chauvet, L.-M. *Du symbolique au symbole* (Paris: Cerf, 1979).

Churches and Business Enterprises in a World of Tension, Church-Business Discussion Group, Zurich, 2nd ed., 1983.

Congar, Y. *Lay People in the Church* (London: Chapman, 1965).

———. *L'ecclésiologie du haut Moyen-Age: De saint Grégoire le Grand à la désunion entre Byzance et Rome* (Paris: Cerf, 1968).

———. *Diversité et communion* (Paris: Cerf, 1982).

———. "Le pape comme patriarche d'occident: Approche d'une réalité trop négligée, *Istina* 28/4 (1983):376-390.

Cousin, H. *L'Evangile de Luc* (Paris: Centurion, 1993).

Dunn, J. D. G. *Baptism in the Holy Spirit* (London: SCM, 1973).

Foulquié, P. and R. Saint-Jean. "Personne," in *Dictionnaire de langue philosophique* (Paris: Presses Universitaires de France, 1962).

Freire, P. *Pedagogy of the Oppressed* (New York: Seabury, 1970).

Gager, J. G. *Kingdom and Community: The Social World of Early Christianity* (Englewood Cliffs, New Jersey: Prentice-Hall, 1975).

Guggenberger, A. "Personne," in *Encyclopédie de la Foi*, Vol. 3 (Paris: Cerf, 1966), pp. 425-437.

Gutiérrez, G. *Las Casas: In Search of the Poor of Jesus Christ.* (Maryknoll, New York: Orbis Books, 1993).

Haenchen, E. *The Acts of the Apostles: A Commentary* (London: Basil Blackwell, 1971).

Hamman, A. "La prière chrétienne et la prière païenne: Formes et différences," in H. Temporini and W. Haase, eds., *Aufstieg und Niedergang der Römischen Welt* (Berlin: Walter der Gruyter, 1980), pp. 1190-1247.

Haulotte, E. "Fondation d'une communauté de type universel: Actes, 10:1-11, 18," *Recherches de Science Religieuse* 58 (1970):63-100.

Initiative Kindugu, "Document on Admission of Guilt," *New People* 29 (March-April 1994).

Johnson, P. *A History of Christianity* (London: Penguin, 1976).

Lecuyer, J. "Libermann et la malédiction de Cham," in P. Coulon et al., *Libermann (1802-1852)* (Paris: Cerf, 1988), pp. 596-608.

Léon-Dufour, X. *Sharing the Eucharistic Bread: The Witness of the New Testament* (New York: Paulist Press, 1987).

Liturgie de l'Eglise particulière et liturgie de l'Eglise universelle. Conférences Saint-Serge, XXXIIIe Semaine d'Etudes liturgiques, Paris, June 30-July 3, 1975 (Rome: Edizioni Liturgiche, 1976).

Lohfink, G. *L'Eglise que voulait Jésus* (Paris: Cerf, 1985).

Meeks, W. A. *The First Urban Christians* (New Haven: Yale University Press, 1983).

Mihevc, J. "The Theology of Structural Adjustment," *Bulletin of Ecumenical Theology* 5/1 (1993):44-60.

Müller, M. and Halder, A. "Person," in K. Rahner, ed., *Encyclopaedia of Theology* (New York: Seabury, 1975), pp. 1206-1213.

Munier C., "Un canon inédit du XXe Concile de Carthage: 'Ut nullus ad Romanam Ecclesiam audeat appellare,' " *Revue des Sciences Religieuses* 40 (1966):113-126.

Pernoud, R., J. Gimpel, and R. Delatouche. *Le Moyen Age pour quoi faire?* (Paris: Editions Stock, 1986).

Philips, G. *L'Eglise et son mystère au IIe Concile du Vatican*, Vol. 1 (Tournai: Desclée, 1967).

Ratzinger, J., and H. Maïer, *Démocratisation dans l'Eglise? Possibilités, limites, risques* (Paris: Apostolat; Québec: Paulines, 1972).

Rengstorf, K. H. "*Apostolos*," in G. Kittel, ed., *Theological Dictionary of the New Testament*, Vol. 1 (Grand Rapids: Eerdmans, 1964), pp. 393-447.

Schillebeeckx, E. *Ministry* (New York: Crossroad, 1981).

———. *Church: The Human Story of God* (New York: Crossroad, 1990).

Schnackenburg, R. *The Gospel according to St. John*, Vol. 1, *Introduction and Commentary on Chapters 1-4*, trans. K. Smyth (London: Burns and Oates, 1968).

———. *The Gospel according to St. John*, Vol. 3 (London: Burns and Oates, 1982).

Thils, G. "Le nouveau code de droit canonique et l'ecclésiologie de Vatican II," *Revue Théologique de Louvain* 14 (1983): 289-301.

———. "Le ministère de Pierre et le service de l' 'unité universelle,' " *Revue Théologique de Louvain* 17 (1986):61-68.

Tillard, J. M. R. *Church of Churches: The Ecclesiology of Communion*

(Collegeville, Minn.: Liturgical Press, 1992).

Tillich, P. *Systematic Theology Studies*, Vol. 3 (Chicago: University of Chicago Press, 1963).

Twohig-Moengangongo, C. "Paradigms of Power," *Bulletin of Ecumenical Theology* 6/1 (1994):33-51.

Vallely, P. *Bad Samaritans: First World Ethics and Third World Debt* (Maryknoll, New York: Orbis Books, 1990).

van Beneden, P. *Aux origines d'une terminologie sacramentelle: Ordo, ordinare, ordinatio dans la littérature chrétienne avant 313* (Louvain: Specilegium Sacrum Lovaniense, 1974).

Vogel, C. "Unité de l'Eglise et pluralité des formes historiques d'organisation ecclésiastique du IIIe au Ve siècle," in Y. Congar and B.-D. Dupuy, eds., *L'Episcopat et l'Eglise universelle* (Paris: Cerf, 1962), pp. 591-636.

Walls, A. F. "Culture and Coherence in Christian History," *Scottish Bulletin of Evangelical Theology* 3/4 (1985).

Weber, M. *The Sociology of Religion* (Boston: Beacon Press, 1963).

Index